100

THINGS TO DO IN

AMARILLO

BEFORE YOU

DIE

100

THINGS TO DO IN
AMARILLO
BEFORE YOU
DIE

ERIC W. MILLER

REEDY PRESS

Library of Congress Control Number: 2021935152

ISBN: 9781681063164

Design by Jill Halpin

All images are courtesy of the author unless otherwise noted.

Printed in the United States of America
21 22 23 24 25   5 4 3 2 1

We (the publisher and the author) have done our best to provide the most accurate information available when this book was completed. However, we make no warranty, guarantee, or promise about the accuracy, completeness, or currency of the information provided, and we expressly disclaim all warranties, express or implied. Please note that attractions, company names, addresses, websites, and phone numbers are subject to change or closure, and this is outside of our control. We are not responsible for any loss, damage, injury, or inconvenience that may occur due to the use of this book. When exploring new destinations, please do your homework before you go. You are responsible for your own safety and health when using this book.

DEDICATION

To everyone, all 7.8 billion inhabitants of planet Earth. We lived through the sadness and tragedy of the COVID-19 pandemic and now approach the future with hope. Let's resume our lives as best we can, while surrounding each other with compassion and love.

To my adopted hometown, Amarillo. It's my pleasure to share your legacy and lore with visitors from all corners of the globe.

To my family. Every one of you makes me a better person.

To my wife, Peggy. Your support is priceless.

CONTENTS

Music and Entertainment

Sports and Recreation

PREFACE

What's COVID-19? And why should I care?

We all asked that in March 2020. The answers are a virus and because it is very contagious. Wearing masks, washing hands, and social distancing were our tools for many months. Vaccines were added in early 2021. It appears we have turned the corner, but a lot is still up in the air.

We are all eager to visit places, to get outside, to see something new. Something like Amarillo. So, while we hope for progress in the COVID-19 fight and an easing to the stranglehold the pandemic has on our lives, that may not be the reality when this book is published in 2021.

I encourage you to double-check each item in this book with respect to COVID-19 safety. Call the attraction or business. Visit their website. Join their email subscription list. Go to the Amarillo Convention & Visitors Bureau (visitamarillo.com) for third-party confirmation. Look at the City of Amarillo's COVID-19 response website (amarilloalerts.com). I am eager to share this information and to promote my hometown, but your health is most important.

ACKNOWLEDGMENTS

It's impossible to acknowledge every single person who helped me with this book. From my first Amarillo boss Jerry Holt to colleagues like DeeDee Poteete, I enjoyed my Texas travel career and things I learned over 20 years ago still help me today. I fell in love with Palo Duro Canyon the first time I saw it in March 1997. Being on the board of Partners in Palo Duro Foundation is icing on the cake. I appreciate the help and feedback from local friends like Stephanie Price, Phyllis Nickum Golden, Daphne Adkins, Gregg Bynum, Wes Reeves, Jason Boyett, Ralph Duke, Eddie Tubbs, Byran Brumley, and Tony Freeman. Historic Route 66 is so important to Amarillo and I must thank Bob Lile, Sonya Lukas and Dora Meroney—who may be the hardest working Route 66 volunteer in the country. Thanks also to Beth Duke, executive director of Center City of Amarillo, and my "go-to" person for anything in Amarillo. Finally, thanks to SATW members and friends Tom Adkinson, Beth D'Addono, Christine Hopkins, Evelyn Kanter, and Cele Seldon, all of them *100 Things to Do* authors in their hometowns, for their encouragement.

FOOD AND DRINK

DEVOUR
A CLASSIC BURGER
AT THE GOLDENLIGHT CAFÉ

The GoldenLight Café on Historic Route 66 claims it is the longest continuously operating restaurant in Amarillo and one of the longest such restaurants on all of Route 66, too. It's easy to taste why. The menu isn't complicated, just burgers, chili, BLTs, chicken sandwiches, fries, rings, tea, soda, and cold beer. Be like a local and grab one of the few spaces at the bar, so you can watch the flattop (probably the same one from 1946) produce row after row of burgers. As the menu reminds everyone, it's not fast food, just good food. Next door is the GoldenLight Cantina, an intimate place for newbies and experienced performers alike. Before COVID-19, it had a robust schedule with live music most Thursday, Friday, and Saturday nights.

GoldenLight Café, 2906 SW 6th Ave., 806-374-9237
goldenlightcafe.com

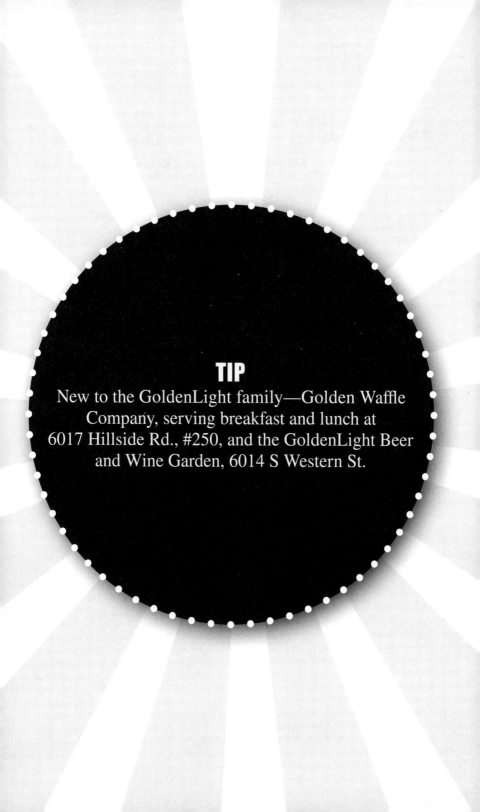

TIP

New to the GoldenLight family—Golden Waffle Company, serving breakfast and lunch at 6017 Hillside Rd., #250, and the GoldenLight Beer and Wine Garden, 6014 S Western St.

FIND FIRE SLICE PIZZERIA
—IT'S WORTH THE EFFORT

A favorite pizzeria is a personal choice. Some folks prefer thin and crispy crusts. Others like a thicker crust. Still others prefer a deep-dish pie. And finally, some enjoy the convenience of delivery from a major chain. It's all here in Amarillo. But my wife and I lean to Fire Slice Pizzeria, a small, homegrown business that, frankly, we have felt both pro and con about. Now, Fire Slice is Amarillo's best pizza. It is thin and bubbly, with a great, crispy crust that comes from its wood-fired oven. Toppings are fresh, cheese is plentiful but not oily, salads are great, and service is friendly. The bar includes lots of wine choices, but we enjoy an ever-increasing list of craft beers, both draft and bottle, local and across the West.

Finding it is the challenge; it is on the back side of the popular Summit Shopping Center at 34th Avenue and Coulter Street. Look for the small signs on either end that point you to the alley, and slowly follow the road—you'll see the crowd of cars and know you're just minutes from a top-notch pizza.

Summit Shopping Center, 7306 SW 34th Ave. (rear), 806-331-2232
fireslice.com

RELAX
WITH A GLASS OF WINE
AT BAR Z WINERY

Local vintner Monty Dixon has been making award-winning wines for years at Bar Z Winery. You won't drive through rows of grapes, but you will find lots of fragrant and rich wines made from grapes grown across the Texas High Plains. His wine list is diverse—cabernet, riesling, tempranillo, pinot noir, pinot grigio, sangiovese, and more. Combine the wine with local bands and custom food trucks on weekends for memorable special events. When the temperature is right, head outdoors to the patio to catch a glimpse of a fiery sunset. It's all on the rim of Palo Duro Canyon. "We left God's landscaping alone," Dixon says.

19290 FM 1541 (S Washington St. in Amarillo city limits), Canyon, TX,
806-488-2214
barzwinery.com

FILL UP
WITH A CHICKEN-FRIED STEAK

Among the pantheon of Texas comfort food, none looms larger than chicken-fried steak (less sophisticated places may call it country-fried steak). Out on the open range, it was a way "Cookie" took a less tender cut of beef and made it appetizing. Now, it is an art form, with restaurants staking their reputations to this dish. This is what they have in common—a large, golden-brown steak that was tenderized, then either deep fried or fried on the flattop, and a large scoop of mashed potatoes on an oval plate, all covered in creamy white gravy. Add a side of green beans (or whatever), some rolls and butter, and iced tea for a traditional comfort experience. Everyone has a personal favorite, aside from Sunday dinner at their mom's. In Amarillo, locals will send you to Youngblood's Café, Green Chile Willy's, Calico County, or Amarillo's Stockyard Grill.

TIP
You'll find a tasty and satisfying chicken-fried steak
at the Big Texan Steak Ranch.

Amarillo's Stockyard Grill
101 S Manhattan St., 806-220-0484
amarillostockyardgrill.com

Calico County
2410 Paramount Blvd., 806-358-7664
calicocountyrestaurant.com

Green Chile Willy's
13651 I-27, 806-622-2200
greenchilewillys.com/Welcome.html

Youngblood's Café
620 SW 16th Ave., 806-342-9411
youngbloodscafe.com

BUZZ AROUND
THE CREEK HOUSE HONEY FARM

It's a honey of an idea—a visit to the area's largest apiary and specialty shop. It's Creek House Honey Farm and Honey Buzz Winery. Owners Paige and George Nester started beekeeping a little over 10 years ago and located their growing business just outside Canyon. Their shop is filled with beekeeping products including a variety of honey, skin-care products, candies, and candles. How about a beehive tour? You'll get the full beekeeping suit for the walk among the buzzing bees. (Tours are only when the bees are active.) Stop in the winery after your tour to celebrate with some mead, a honey-based alcoholic beverage that goes back thousands of years. They have lots of other selections if mead seems too sweet.

5005 4th Ave., Canyon, TX, 806-381-3446
creekhousehoneyfarm.com

USE YOUR CHOPSTICKS
AT LEMONGRASS SUSHI & WOK

Sushi is here on the high plains. It's in restaurants, supermarkets, and small neighborhood stores. My wife and I have tried more than our share, and we always come back to Lemongrass. It's in a strip center along Western Street and qualifies as a small, family-run eatery. The 10 tables and half-dozen booths are always full, and the sushi is always fresh. Sit at the bar and watch the orders being made. We like the tempura rolls; the batter is light and quickly fried. A couple of our favorites, like the Western Crossing and the Flying Dragon, with a couple beers are very reasonably priced, leaving money to head out on the town. Regardless of the selection, we have never been disappointed. Takeout and delivery services, too.

2207 S Western St., 806-352-5535
lemongrass-sushi-wok.business.site/?utm_source=gmb&utm_medium=referral

FANCY A DONUT
FROM HOUSE OF DONUTS

Is it doughnut or donut? Regardless, these sweet, doughy concoctions have developed a high-end personality in recent years. More than the classic cake donut and a cup of coffee for breakfast, they have become culinary statements, appropriate all day. Toppings run the gamut from sprinkles and sugary glaze to bacon, Oreos, gumdrops, Ferrero Rocher candy, and much more. Amarillo's entry is House of Donuts, a small storefront tucked away on the city's northeast side, just past the Tri-State Fairgrounds. They start early (5 a.m.) and are there until 2 p.m. or when they sell out. There are always lots of traditional choices, as well as a few specialty choices. Have something special in mind for the office or home? Let the owner know—he may just hit a custom home-run.

1615 N Grand St., 806-803-0845
house-of-donuts-donut-shop.business.site/

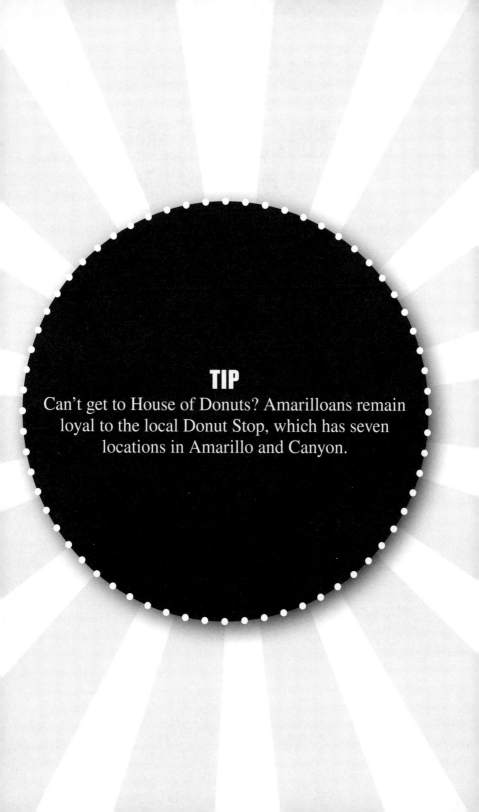

TIP

Can't get to House of Donuts? Amarilloans remain loyal to the local Donut Stop, which has seven locations in Amarillo and Canyon.

GET HALFWAY THERE
AT THE MIDPOINT CAFÉ

Route 66 is 2,448 miles long, from Chicago, Illinois, to Santa Barbara, California. But at only one spot can you say, "We're halfway there." That spot is Adrian, Texas, about 45 miles west of Amarillo. And that landmark is the Midpoint Café. It's a '50s-style pit stop that's home to great food, a Route 66 gift shop (naturally), and the only place to get Ugly Pie. The crust may not be perfect (it started life called Ugly Crust Pie), but it tastes divine. Local bakers keep a wide array of flavors fresh daily. The café is popular with groups traveling Route 66 (motorcycles, classic cars, RVs), so while you wait, step across Historic Route 66 for the photo op—the sign makes sure everyone knows precisely where you are. On the way to or from Adrian, pull over in Vega, Texas, to see the Milburn-Price Culture Museum—its Dust Bowl stories are amazing. Don't miss the restored Magnolia Gas Station across the highway.

Midpoint Café

305 W Historic Rte. 66, Adrian, TX, 806-538-6379

facebook.com/MidpointCafe

Milburn-Price Culture Museum

1005 Coke St., Vega, TX, 806-676-7169

facebook.com/Milburn-Price-Culture-Museum-1448761355376339

Magnolia Gas Station

105 S Main St., Vega, TX

KEEP COOL
ON THE PATIO OF IT'S A PUNJABI AFFAIR

Patio dining, while already popular, took on a new, safer shine during the pandemic. People looked more and more for places outside, just not at their homes, as alternatives for dining out. Amarillo has its share, but none with the spice of It's a Punjabi Affair, a top-flight Indian restaurant that has been making lots of noise through apps and social media. Walk up to the window, and chances are you'll talk with the owner, TJ, or his wife, Mauli. They prepare all the Indian fare standards, but he'll tell you what's best that day. My fave is Nahk-Rah Naan. Get it to go or find a table on the small, enclosed patio that is winterized to permit eating when temperatures get a little cooler. After dinner, head east on Historic Route 66 to catch some live music.

4201 Bushland Blvd., 806-414-2114
itsapunjabiaffair.square.site/

SAVOR SOME SMOKY MEAT
AT TYLER'S BARBEQUE

Truth is, not too long ago, the Texas Panhandle was a barbecue desert. Aside from ribs, Amarillo residents just didn't have the opportunity to enjoy the moist, smoked, sliced brisket and other standards that graced plates downstate. Thankfully, that's changed, led by our own member of the Texas Monthly Top 50 Barbecue Joints, Tyler's Barbeque. It's all here—brisket, ribs, sausage, sides, what you expect from a top Texas pit master. Local newspaper columnist Jon Mark Beilue found someone who ate here every day. If you can't do that, come on Thursday when you can get the green chili mac 'n' cheese on the side. Another good barbecue choice—Spicy Mike's Bar-B-Q Haven (6723 S Western). Go early: both places sell out regularly.

3301 Olsen Blvd., 806-331-2271
tylersbarbeque.com

LOOK FOR FELDMAN'S WRONG WAY DINER
IN CANYON

Looking around for a place to eat in Canyon? Bring your castaways (friends and family) to relax and eat at Feldman's Wrong Way Diner. Whatever you order, there is no wrong way about it; it will be good. A Canyon landmark for 20 years, now across from West Texas A&M University, it is full of good burgers, salads, catfish, soup and, of course, chicken-fried steak. There's a nice relief of The Lighthouse from Palo Duro Canyon State Park along a main wall in the dining room. You can't miss the large-scale model railroad hanging from the ceiling that makes its way through the entire restaurant. Look for the original script from *Gilligan's Island* framed behind the front welcome counter; Wrong-Way Feldman was a character on that popular 1960s sitcom.

2100 N 2nd Ave., Canyon, TX, 806-655-2700
feldmansdiner.com

EAT A STEAK (WHAT ELSE?)
AT THE BIG TEXAN STEAK RANCH

Everyone thinks they cook/grill/broil the best steaks. Me too. But I don't attempt to grill the ultimate steak—the 72-ounce steak that is part of the Big Texan Steak Ranch challenge. Eat the steak—it's top sirloin—and the entire dinner (shrimp cocktail, baked potato, salad, and roll) in under an hour, and it is free. Can't finish? It will cost you $72, still a bargain. They'll also give you the ultimate doggie bag. Nearly 10,000 have finished the steak; women are more successful than men. The reigning champ is a young lady who ate three complete dinners in 20 minutes, no doggie bag needed, in 2015. Don't want to try the challenge? Their menu is full of options for breakfast, lunch, or dinner. Go for a large rib eye, the chicken-fried steak, or some prime rib, and you won't be disappointed. Seating is on long tables, so your dining partners may be from around the world. The main dining room fills up quickly, especially in the evening, so plan your visit accordingly.

7701 I-40 E, 806-372-6000
bigtexan.com

GRILL YOUR DINNER NOT IN THE BACKYARD,
BUT AT BRACERO'S MEXICAN GRILL & BAR

With dozens of Mexican restaurants in Amarillo, it's hard to single out one. If you're looking for something authentic but with a twist, consider Bracero's Mexican Grill & Bar. The Historic Route 66 location is in a vintage gas station, renovated and repurposed as a restaurant. The main dining room is friendly, the patrons are lively, and the entertainment (generally a two- or three-piece group) is authentic. So, it is not a quiet, romantic hideaway. But the food is genuine. Portions are big. The menu is exhausting, with more selections than you could ever try. If your group is large, or maybe it's just your appetite, think about the parrillada, a combination of meats (beef, goat, quail, chicken, or lamb) or fish right off the grill. A more traditional selection might be the fish tacos. It's an evening like no other in town—the line out the door on weekends attests to that.

2822 SW 6th Ave., 806-220-2395
braceroson6thst.com

TIP

By year's end, Bracero's Mexican Grill & Bar will have a downtown location in the old Cizon's Jewelry building on Polk Street.

DINE
AROUND THE WORLD
ALONG EAST AMARILLO BOULEVARD

You may think Amarillo is a "bed and burger" town—not much to choose from for dining options. Get off the interstate and head to East Amarillo Boulevard, a bustling four-mile neighborhood between US 87/287 and state highway 335 that is the ethnic center of Amarillo. Dining options? West of the railroad overpass near Grand Street, it is mostly Mexican, while east of the overpass, it is mostly Asian (China, Thailand, Vietnam, Japan, Laos, and Myanmar). Head far enough east on Amarillo Boulevard, and you will find a Somali restaurant, too. Don't overlook the various food markets, panaderias, tortillerias, and carnicerias that dot this stretch of the boulevard—they are caretakers of authentic ingredients from around the globe. It is a great food adventure. Amidst it all remains the Cattleman's Café—a 24-hour, comfort-food purveyor in the same location since the 1940s. This was the original alignment of Route 66, so you'll also see a lot of references to the Mother Road, too.

Check out Google Maps for the best listing of all the dining and food shopping options along the boulevard: google.com/maps/place/E+Amarillo+Blvd,+Texas.

Some of the businesses along East Amarillo Boulevard include:

Aye San Bu Myanmar Market
5619 E Amarillo Blvd., 806-331-5325

Blue Sky Asian Market
5631 E Amarillo Blvd., 806-331-5065

Dong Phoung Oriental Food
2218 E Amarillo Blvd., 806-371-0914

El Manantial
3823 E Amarillo Blvd., 806-383-1852

El Tropico
1111 E Amarillo Blvd., 806-371-0226

La Mariscada Seafood
3500 E Amarillo Blvd., 806-584-9472

La Super Carniceria
1011 N Buchanan St., 806-220-0378

Ly's Café
5615 E Amarillo Blvd., 806-383-1569

Panaderia Sanchez
1010 E Amarillo Blvd., 806-371-7757

Sinaloa Hot Dogs & Mexican Food
2618 E Amarillo Blvd., 806-367-8935

Somali African Safari Restaurant
5945 E Amarillo Blvd., 806-471-0490

Tacos Garcia
2200 E Amarillo Blvd., 806-342-9310

Tan Phat Market
5321 E Amarillo Blvd., 806-322-3669

Thai Star
3800 E Amarillo Blvd., 806-383-4727

QUAFF A BEER
AT AMARILLO'S CRAFT BREWERS

For years, Amarillo was a company town, if the companies were Coors, Budweiser, and Miller. But local craft brewing has exploded in Amarillo. Looking for a place to enjoy a local brew? Here are four: The Big Texan Brewery (yes, that Big Texan), Long Wooden Spoon Brewing (maybe the oldest craft brewer in town), Six Car Pub & Brewery, and Pondaseta Brewing. Each has a specialty, and certainly the Big Texan has a small advantage—it's in the Big Texan Steak Ranch. All the brewers are serious, have brought home an award or two, and have developed loyal followings. Some of the locally named brews, each a distinctive take on a brewing classification, are Bomb City Bock at the Big Texan, 6th Street Wheat at Long Wooden Spoon, Sud Puddles at Six Car Pub, and I-40 IPA at Pondaseta. There are so many more brews to choose from. If you really want one of the national big boys . . . well, that's your choice.

Big Texan Brewery
7701 I-40 E, 806-372-6000
bigtexan.com/big-texan-brewery-amarillo-texas/

Long Wooden Spoon Brewing
4098 Business Park Dr., 806-553-0397
lwsbrewing.com

Six Car Pub & Brewery
625 S Polk St., 806-576-3396
sixcarpub.com

Pondaseta Brewing Company
7500 SW 45th Ave., 806-418-6282
pondaseta.com

FEAST ON SEAFOOD
AT SAM'S SOUTHERN EATERY

Sam's has been getting lots of social splash in Amarillo since opening in 2020. Great catfish. Top-notch seafood. Comfort food like fried green tomatoes, po'boys, crab cakes, and livers and gizzards (it doesn't taste like chicken, but give it a try). It checks all the boxes for good food, large portions, and great service. The atmosphere is limited (the building was a Burger King at one time), but who cares—you can't eat atmosphere. Amarillo loves going local, so imagine the surprise of learning it is part of a chain. Started in Louisiana, it has outposts in 12 states, including as far north as Ohio. But it's only the Amarillo location that concerns us.

4317 Teckla Blvd., 806-437-1349
samssouthernamarillo.com

TIP

Since you're in the neighborhood, consider Scott's Oyster Bar at 4150 Paramount Blvd. The small building casts a large shadow in the local dining scene.

SIP SOME JOE
AT AMARILLO'S LOCAL COFFEE SHOPS

Amarillo loves its local businesses, and none are more loved than its local coffee shops. Roasters was the first. Then came, in no special order, Palace, Cliffside, The 806, S&J, Five Senses, and Strata. Each has its own vibe. Roasters is established with longtime coffee klatches, Palace has a wide professional appeal, Cliffside specializes in top-notch, drive-through coffee, The 806 is funky and features local artists on the wall (look for the turntable checkout), S&J is a downtown location, Five Senses awakens all your senses, and Strata serves the medical center. For all the popularity of local coffee, there are still several very popular Starbucks shops in town, all of them routinely packed, too.

So, finding a good cup of coffee is no problem in Amarillo.

Roasters Coffee & Tea
1818 S Georgia St., 806-331-6563
4709 S Bell St., 806-350-7460
3429 S Soncy Rd., 806-331-5523
6014 Lowes Lane, 806-350-2889
roasters.biz

Palace Coffee Company
7304 SW 34th Ave.
817 S Polk St.
420 15th St., Canyon, TX
806-476-0111 (all locations)
palacecoffee.co

The 806 Coffee + Lounge
2812 SW 6th Ave., 806-322-1806
the806.com

Cliffside Coffee
2540 Ross-Osage Dr., 806-731-6239
SW 45th Ave. & Teckla Blvd., 806-414-2446
4167 SW 34th Ave., 806-350-7906
cliffsidecoffee.com

S&J Coffee House
600 S Tyler St., 806-705-1397
sandjcoffeehouse.com

Five Senses Coffee House
6010 S Western St., 806-803-5100
fivesensescoffeehouse.com

Strata Coffee Bar
7560 Outlook Dr., 806-350-8385
stratacoffeebar.com

DRINK THE VODKA
AT BOMB CITY DISTILLERY

Ever seen a bottle that looks like that before? It looks like a small bomb. It's filled with the purest, freshest vodka produced. Bomb City Distillery is Amarillo's first and only distillery, dedicated to crafting the finest spirits possible. The ultra-premium vodka is distilled 12 times from top-notch grain to yield the smoothest product possible. Twelve times? You bet. Stop by the distillery for tasting hours (Friday and Saturday from 4–11 p.m.), and put them to the test. Chances are one of Amarillo's favorite food trucks will also be on-site. Bomb City Vodka is also available at several local liquor stores.

306 S Cleveland St., 806-220-BOMB (2662)
bombcitydistillery.com

TIP
Why is Amarillo Bomb City?

Because it is home to the Pantex Plant, a vital cog in the nation's nuclear arms program since the 1950s. Located about 15 miles northeast of Amarillo, Pantex was originally an assembly plant but is dedicated more and more to the disassembly and safe storage of components of the US nuclear arms stockpile. As a major national security site, the plant and its grounds are strictly controlled and off-limits to all civilians.

Other "Bomb City" businesses you may find include Bomb City Kitchen, Bomb City Safes, Bomb City Dent Repair, Bomb City Ink and Bomb City Custom Motorcycles.

MUSIC
AND ENTERTAINMENT

LAUGH AND CRY
AT THE AMARILLO LITTLE THEATRE

Little in name only, the Amarillo Little Theatre (ALT) is one of the nation's oldest community theater troupes. Shows highlight the wide array of acting and artistic talent in the Amarillo area. Each season includes seven or eight different productions. Big musicals, comedies, and dramas are staged primarily on the Main Stage. The Adventure Space hosts cutting-edge pieces that are frequently more appropriate for adult audiences. Academy shows, featuring teenagers and younger actors, can be some of the most popular and enjoyable offerings. Regardless what show you choose, ALT actors and technical staff will impress. ALT quickly implemented COVID-19 protocols to ensure the health of patrons and actors.

2019 Civic Cir. (Main Stage)
2751 Civic Cir. (Adventure Space), 806-355-9991
amarillolittletheatre.org

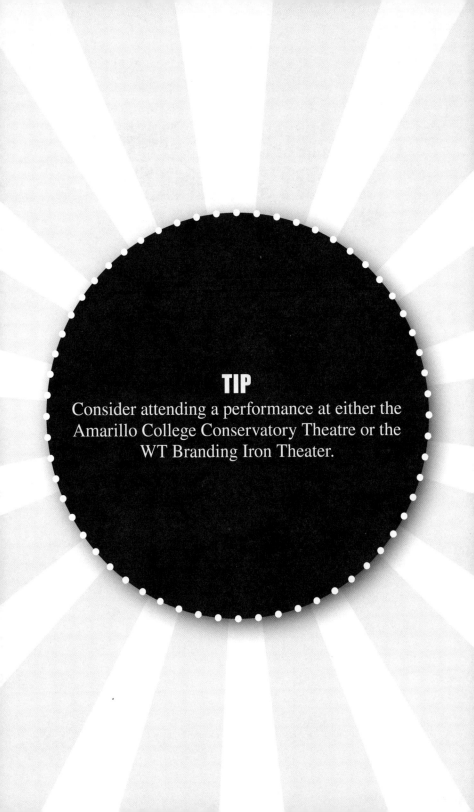

TIP
Consider attending a performance at either the Amarillo College Conservatory Theatre or the WT Branding Iron Theater.

DANCE TO YOUR HEART'S CONTENT
WITH THE LONE STAR BALLET

We're not talking about boot-scootin' the Texas two-step at an Amarillo dance hall, which you can certainly do. It's about the ballet and the professional dance troupe that has been on the Amarillo arts scene for years. The Lone Star Ballet (LSB), founded in 1975, is a cultural force. The season routinely includes three or four professional performances at the Globe-News Center for the Performing Arts, including a beloved annual performance of The Nutcracker. Offstage, the LSB offers academy classes in ballet, tap, jazz, and modern dance at locations in Amarillo and across the Texas Panhandle. Guest dancers and artists from around the world frequently participate in the performances and the academy classes. Don't think ballet is for you? LSB is the perfect way to enjoy a first ballet or dance performance; you may like what you see.

3218 Hobbs Rd., 806-372-2463
lonestarballet.org

LISTEN TO AMARILLO
DURING A *HEY AMARILLO!* PODCAST

Here's something to do once a week from your home, office, car, or just about anywhere: listen to the *Hey Amarillo!* podcast, a series of interviews with members of the Amarillo community who make this place so interesting. Creator Jason Boyett started in 2017 with a basic idea—create a weekly 30-minute interview with a person of interest. The interview focuses on their likes and dislikes, as well as their hopes and dreams for this city of 200,000-plus. In this age of inclusion, Boyett has done a great job bridging differences to promote understanding. *Hey Amarillo!* has thousands of monthly listeners, several sponsors, and even a fledgling beer festival with partner the Big Texan. Some of the interviewees include *Two For The Road* co-host Nikki Green, Amarillo weatherman-turned-educator-turned-local-historian Paul Matney, COVID-19 frontline caregiver Dr. Kishore Yalamanchili, and many others. Find *Hey Amarillo!* wherever you look for podcasts, and subscribe to its weekly email newsletter.

heyamarillo.com

ENJOY
CONCERTS AND EVENTS
AT STARLIGHT RANCH

One of the brightest new lights on the Amarillo music scene is Starlight Ranch, the Big Texan's foray into concerts and special events. The outdoor facility was voted Amarillo's number one music venue in 2018, 2019, and 2020, attracting large crowds for great musical acts in a relaxed outdoor setting. Special events, like the *Hey Amarillo!* Beer Festival in 2019, added to the schedule. A bevy of family activities, such as a maze, playground, and Putt-Putt golf course all out back and a zip line overhead, mean Starlight has something for everybody. Starlight producers are optimistic that the 2021 season will be successful and are confident full activity will return in 2022. Keep track of events online, by social media, or with an email subscription.

1415 Sunrise Dr., 806-556-4456
bigtexan.com/starlight-ranch-event-center

PILE IN THE CAR
AND HEAD TO
TASCOSA DRIVE-IN THEATER

Going to the movies has been tough during the COVID-19 pandemic. Here's a way to enjoy a film with the entire family—go to Amarillo's Tascosa Drive-In Theater. It's a vanishing breed in this complicated entertainment industry. But the Tascosa Drive-In, one of a couple dozen drive-ins remaining in Texas, caters to purists who still love to see a flick on a BIG screen. Each night is a double feature, frequently with first-run movies, starting a little after sunset. Go Texan and drive a pickup to the movies and set up lawn chairs in the truck bed. The season is from early spring through Halloween, weather permitting. Like all good drive-ins, the Tascosa has a playground next to the single screen and a great concession stand.

1999 Dumas Dr., 806-383-3882
tascosadrivein.com

ENJOY THE MIDWAY
AT THE TRI-STATE FAIR

Think of a county fair, complete with rides, crafts, livestock shows, beauty queens, fair food, concerts, and the largest pumpkin or biggest tomato contest. Maybe you're too young to remember. Change that at Amarillo's Tri-State Fair and Rodeo, a nine-day celebration held over two weekends in the middle of September every year that attracts more than 100,000 fairgoers. The Tri-State Fair kicks off with a parade in downtown Amarillo. The Professional Rodeo Cowboys Association rodeo runs for three nights at the end of the fair, always with top-flight musical entertainment after each rodeo performance. And the midway is packed with some of the best rides around. The 2020 fair was cancelled due to COVID-19, but organizers are optimistic for 2021 (September 17–25), 2022, and beyond.

3301 SE 10th Ave., 806-376-7767
tristatefair.com

SOAR
WITH THE AMARILLO SYMPHONY

What has over 85 members, has been contributing to the arts scene for more than 95 years, and has its home in a world-class performance venue? The Amarillo Symphony. Performance weekends are a calendar highlight from September through May. The Amarillo Symphony repertoire presents the power of music, from classic composers to cutting-edge modern musicians. A concert in the Globe-News Center for the Performing Arts, with its outstanding acoustics, will be a highlight of your visit. While tickets are frequently sold out, check with the symphony office to see if tickets are available for a Friday or Saturday night concert when you are in town. If the symphony is not performing, ask about more intimate performances by Chamber Music Amarillo.

301 S Polk St., 806-376-8782
amarillosymphony.org

RIDE THE TEXAS TORNADO
AT WONDERLAND AMUSEMENT PARK

The climb to the top of the Texas Tornado, a fast, steel roller coaster at Wonderland Amusement Park, may be the tallest man-made hill in the Texas Panhandle. You can see for miles from the top . . . but only for a second before you're off on a speedy, double-loop roller coaster that rivals big-park thrill machines. Overall, there are five roller coasters in Wonderland, making it one of the best collections of coasters around—the American Coaster Association says so! With lots of water rides, there are plenty of chances to get wet on hot summer days. Right next door is the Wonderland Miniature Golf Course, a great addition to the park experience. And it's just a fraction of the price of big-city theme parks. An all-day weekend Ultimate WOW pass to Wonderland is just $39. Better yet, the park's smaller size makes it easy to get around, the lines are very manageable, and getting lost just isn't a problem.

2601 Dumas Dr., 806-383-3344
wonderlandpark.com

TIP
Find a $2 coupon on the Wonderland website.

LISTEN TO SUMMER MUSIC FESTIVALS
IN AMARILLO AND CANYON

Outdoor music is a great way to relax in the evening with friends and neighbors. A summer visitor has access to several music series, many at no cost.

High Noon on the Square is Wednesday at noon in front of the Potter County Courthouse from June to August. Music is free, and lunch is about $7, or bring your own.

Starlight Theater is run by the city of Amarillo and is on the outdoor stage in Sam Houston Park every Tuesday evening, from June into August. Free.

June Jazz is just that. Weekly Tuesday evening concerts in June on the campus of Amarillo College feature the area's best jazz musicians. Free. In October, look for Jazztober, another free weekly jazz series on Tuesday night at the Bivins Mansion.

Music in the Gardens, on Thursday evenings at the Amarillo Botanical Gardens, features top local and regional talent for a nominal entrance fee (free if you're a member of the Amarillo Botanical Gardens).

All the series operated to some extent in 2021 and look to full returns in 2022.

High Noon on the Square
806-372-6744

Starlight Theater
806-378-9391

June Jazz
806-371-5340

Music in the Gardens
806-352-6513

TIP
Check with Canyon's Main Street organization about
their summer music series on the square.

SNAP YOUR FINGERS TO LIVE MUSIC
ALONG HISTORIC ROUTE 66

Local and regional bands have learned that crowds of music fans await them in clubs up and down Amarillo's Historic Route 66. Indoors or out (when the weather cooperates), eager audiences listen to country, western, rock, pop, folk, jazz, and even classical music along Sixth Avenue, between Georgia and Western streets. Check out places like Smokey Joe's, GoldenLight Cantina, Broken Spoke, Leftwoods, Skooterz, Handle Bar & Grill, or the Fibonacci Building (home to Chamber Music Amarillo). Need help finding the right location for your musical taste? Facebook's Amarillo Music Scene does a good job of tracking live music across the city. Or, just drive along Historic Route 66 with your car windows down and ears wide open!

facebook.com/amarillomusicscene

HAS THE FAT LADY SUNG?
FIND THE ANSWER AT AMARILLO OPERA

What a horrible thing to say or write. For many, this is the description of opera. But opera is so much more. In Amarillo, the best place to learn that is Amarillo Opera (AO). The company has performed some of history's best operas, including *La Boheme, Die Fledermaus, Rigoletto* and *Madame Butterfly.* AO has also performed more modern versions of operatic music, such as the popular musical hit *Les Misérables,* as well as hosted an all-comers community performance of Handel's "Hallelujah" chorus. AO is dedicated to developing the next generation of operatic talent through an impressive list of young artist mentoring and outreach programs. Most AO performances are in the Globe-News Center for the Performing Arts, where the world-class acoustics enhance both the audience and performer experience. Attend the AO, and you won't say any more about the fat lady singing.

2223 S Van Buren St., 806-372-7464
amarilloopera.org

SUBSCRIBE
TO THE WEEKLY EVENT EMAIL: *AMARILLO*

It's a question that lingers—what is there to do this weekend? Of course, you are reading this book, which has lots of great ideas, but what about those special, one-time highlights put on by galleries, museums, restaurants, craft breweries, music venues, and much more? The place to keep up to date for the weekend is *AMarillo,* a weekly email from the Amarillo Convention & Visitors Bureau. For more than five years, *AMarillo* has kept track of local events. It's free and comes to your email box on Tuesday morning, with a score of ideas for the coming weekend. It's easy to sign up—go to visitamarillo.com/about-amarillo/travel-guides/newsletter/. Speaking of emails, most every organization listed in this book has an email newsletter, some with admission or weekly specials. Feel free to sign up—they are free—and reap the rewards.

1000 S Polk St., 806-374-1497
visitamarillo.com

TIP
Ask the Amarillo CVB about the new Panhandle Savings Pass.

SING ALONG
AT THE WOODY GUTHRIE
FOLK MUSIC CENTER

Drive an hour from Amarillo to find the home of a musical legend and the folk foundation of the entire US: Woody Guthrie. Yes, that Woody Guthrie. Musician, artist, author, and so much more. He lived in Pampa, Texas, during the Great Depression and the Dust Bowl, working in the Harris Drug Store but performing, writing, and giving thousands (maybe millions) of people hope during some dark times. The Woody Guthrie Folk Music Center celebrates his creativity, not only because of "This Land Is Your Land," a classic song we all learned in elementary school, but all 3,000 songs he penned over his career. Friday evening open mic events attract musicians from across the region as well as an occasional national or international artist. Build a Woody playlist, and sing along during your drive.

320 S Cuyler, Pampa, TX, 806-665-0883
woodyguthriepampatx.com

SPORTS
AND RECREATION

SEARCH FOR HISTORY
IN ALIBATES FLINT QUARRIES
NATIONAL MONUMENT

Tucked away in a corner of Lake Meredith National Recreation Area is one of the most historically significant locations in the Texas Panhandle. The Alibates Flint Quarries National Monument honors and remembers the people who used this location to quarry the valuable Alibates Flint. It was vital for tools and weapons of all kinds, perhaps by mammoth hunters 13,000 years ago. The flint became part of an early trade network reaching across what we now call the Great Plains. Ask about petroglyphs in the monument that date to the Antelope Creek people about 900 years ago. It's best to check the schedule and join a hike with a park ranger to explore the quarries. Come in late spring for a chance to see fields of native wildflowers.

Lake Meredith National Recreation Area Headquarters
419 E Broadway, Fritch, TX, 806-857-6680
nps.gov/lamr/index.htm

Alibates Flint Quarries Visitor Center
37084 Alibates Rd., Fritch, TX
nps.gov/alfl/index.htm

SPLASH ALL DAY
AT CANYON'S AQUA PARK

The rage in water fun is a water park. It has a wading pool, a large main pool, water slides, diving boards, a lazy river, and lots of special features to help you get, and stay, wet. Canyon has opened the Canyon Aqua Park (CAP), and it checks all the boxes. Get admission tickets through the web site. The CAP also stresses social distancing and thorough sanitation throughout the park. More than 30,000 people have flocked to the CAP each summer since its 2017 opening.

1900 12th Ave., Canyon, TX, 806-655-5016
canyontx.com/347/Canyon-Aqua-Park---The-CAP

TIP
While in Canyon's Connor Park, look for the Sad Monkey Railroad. It's on display after years of service in Palo Duro Canyon State Park.

CATCH THE FRIDAY NIGHT LIGHTS
OF HIGH SCHOOL FOOTBALL

In Amarillo, high school sports reign, and football is king. Fans for a big Amarillo high school or a small-town high school think nothing of driving a 400-mile round trip for a game. The Stratford Elks and Wellington Skyrockets are perennial state powers, capturing small-school titles in recent years. Six-man football, reserved for the smallest schools in the state, has great popularity in towns like Happy and Groom. Large-school rivalries, like Amarillo versus Tascosa, pack the city's 15,000-seat stadium to the brim. Consider spending a fall Friday night (occasionally a Thursday) under the lights with some football-mad residents. Not here during football season? Basketball (boys' and girls') and girls' volleyball are very popular across the area, with some schools bringing back state championships year after year.

Dick Bivins Stadium
(Amarillo, Caprock, Palo Duro, and Tascosa high schools)
801 S Marrs St., 806-326-1102
amaisd.org/488349_3

Happy State Bank (formerly Kimbrough) Stadium
(Canyon and Randall high schools)
2800 N 23rd St., Canyon, TX, 806-677-2600
canyonisd.net/departments/athletics/

SWIM
AND SO MUCH MORE
AT LAKE MEREDITH
NATIONAL RECREATION AREA

Boaters wanting a quick trip don't have many choices in Amarillo. One has always been Lake Meredith, a 10,000-acre lake about 35 miles northeast of Amarillo. But it is so much more. Thanks to the sprawling Lake Meredith National Recreation Area (LMNRA) surrounding the lake, it's a place to camp, picnic, hike, mountain bike, sail, ride ATVs, fish, and hunt (on a limited basis). You can even kayak in the cattails and slow water just below the dam. There are probably other great things to do—just ask the friendly National Park Service staff assigned to LMNRA. Yes, you can swim there, too. Remember, they take water safety seriously—and you should, too.

419 E Broadway, Fritch, TX, 806-857-3151
nps.gov/lamr/index.htm

SWING A CLUB
AT THE PUBLIC GOLF COURSES

Amarillo is blessed with four great public golf courses. Each one is a challenge, and each one is a great value. Comanche Trail Golf Complex in southeast Amarillo beckons to the links-style player. Both Tomahawk and Arrowhead courses encourage the bump-and-run style of links play. On the north side of Amarillo, you will find two more traditional courses as part of the Ross Rogers Golf Complex. Mustang is the original course that has been revamped completely, and WildHorse opened to rave reviews in 2004. Each complex has a full-line pro shop as well as friendly, talented staff available for lessons. Regardless of your choice, it will be a great value, with greens fees never topping $30 for a round of golf (cart rentals extra). With over 270 days of sunshine a year, and mild temperatures even in the winter, Amarillo is a fine choice for golf.

Ross Rogers Golf Complex
722 NW 24th Ave., 806-378-3086
playgolfamarillo.com/ross-rogers

Comanche Trails Golf Complex
4200 S Grand St., 806-378-4281
playgolfamarillo.com/comanche-trail

TIP

Canyon has a popular public course, too:
Palo Duro Creek Golf Course.

ZIP ACROSS A CANYON,
THANKS TO PALO DURO CANYON ZIP LINE & ADVENTURE PARK

Zip lines are very popular. They cross lakes, fly through forest canopies and even soar over Fremont Street in Las Vegas. But a zip line crossing a canyon? It's here, just south of Amarillo. Palo Duro Canyon Zip Line & Adventure Park lets you zip 300 feet above a side canyon to Palo Duro Canyon. Look to your right during the fast trip for a great view into Palo Duro Canyon State Park—which reaches up to 800 feet deep. Regular admission lets you fly the canyon a couple of times, so you really have an impression of its majesty. Better yet, the zip line (a private attraction) is located just outside the main entrance to Palo Duro Canyon State Park. Can't get a campsite in the state park? Ask about camping at Palo Duro Zip Line.

11100 TX Hwy. 217, Canyon, TX, 806-488-2260
palodurozip.com

GO TO THE BLUFF
AT WILDCAT BLUFF NATURE CENTER

Unfortunately, many locals may not know about Wildcat Bluff Nature Center. It covers a section of land (640 acres) from the historic Frying Pan Ranch on the western boundary of Amarillo. It is the fabled location of the last wildcat believed to live in Potter County—hence, Wildcat Bluff. It has a good loop of trails, from the nature center to a working windmill to the bluff and back to the nature center. It's up to five miles of trails. Libb's Trail is a short, paved trail for those needing an easier path. Trails are open sunrise to sunset; the buildings are open on a very flexible schedule. There is a nominal fee suggested for hiking—you can pay in the well-marked box on the patio. I took a small group of travel writers here for a sunrise hike, and it remains a highlight for them. In the summer, afternoon temperatures routinely approach 100 degrees, so carry plenty of water with you.

2301 N Soncy Rd., 806-352-6007
wildcatbluff.org

SPEED AROUND THE OVAL
AT ROUTE 66 MOTOR SPEEDWAY

Saturday night at the track—there's nothing like it. Amarillo's version, Route 66 Motor Speedway, has been attracting drivers and fans for decades. The high-banked, 3/8-mile dirt oval hosts weekly races and big crowds from May to September. Competitors include United States Racing Association Modifieds, Limited Modifieds, and Tuners; quite likely, the talent you see sliding through the curves may be headed to the major leagues of racing—perhaps to NASCAR. Gates open at 5:30 p.m., and racing starts at 7 p.m. Ask about pit pass availability. It costs a bit more but puts you in the middle of the action.

4101 TX 335 Loop, 806-335-3478
route66motorspeedway.net

TIP
More of a straight-line fan? Amarillo Dragway (12955 Burlington Rd.) has a summer schedule for professional and amateur drivers.

SPOT A SOD POODLE
AT HODGETOWN

Chances are, you have no idea what a sod poodle is. Folks in Amarillo know sod poodle is a fancy name for a prairie dog. It is also the mascot of Amarillo's AA baseball team. An affiliate of the Arizona Diamondbacks, the Sod Poodles play in the 10-team Double-A Central League. Their home games are played in Hodgetown, the city's three-year-old baseball stadium in downtown. Games are well-attended, but tickets are usually available, so check the website or stop by the Hodgetown box office. Look for seats on the third-base side—they are in the shade the entire game, a benefit on a summer evening. Stop by the Sod Poodles store; their unusual mascot, one of the most popular in the minor leagues, drives sales worldwide.

715 S Buchanan St., 806-803-9547
milb.com/amarillo

DIVE IN
AN AMARILLO PUBLIC POOL

When it's 100 degrees outside, a swimming pool feels very good. The city of Amarillo has four options for the visitor. Southwest and Southeast parks each has a large outdoor pool with a diving area, water slides, and features. The Charles Warford Activity Center has an indoor pool. The Thompson Park pool is getting a complete facelift that will make it the largest public aquatic facility in the area. Thompson Park will include a lazy river, cabanas, and a main pool area for 400 guests. All the pools are handicapped-accessible. The outdoor pools are open Memorial Day to late August, and the Warford Center pool is open year-round. Fees for all the pools are very reasonable. Ask about special evening hours.

TIP

For young families, there are 13 splash pads in parks around the city. They are free and open daily during the swimming season. For more splash pad information, call City of Amarillo Parks & Recreation at 806-378-3036.

Southeast Park Pool
3435 S Osage St., 806-378-6007

Southwest Park Pool
4850 S Bell St., 806-378-6007

Thompson Park Pool
2401 Dumas Dr., 806-378-6007

Warford Activity Center Pool
1330 NW 18th Ave., 806-378-6007
amarilloparks.org/programs-events/aquatics/pools

PRACTICE YOUR SERVE
AT THE AMARILLO NATIONAL TENNIS CENTER

The Amarillo National Tennis Center is a complete tennis facility with 14 lighted outdoor courts and three indoor courts; all of them are compliant with the Americans with Disabilities Act. Professional staff offer group classes and private lessons for juniors and adults, beginner to advanced player. Tournaments and leagues cater to all levels of play, stressing a competitive spirit on the court while emphasizing the pure exercise value of the sport for all players. Kids Inc. and the Alex O'Brien Foundation have teamed up to make the sport and the center's programs affordable to all young players.

5000 S Bell St., 806-359-2090
amarilloparks.org/programs-events/tennis

TIP
Ask about the six pickleball courts added to the facility in response to the growing popularity of the racquet sport.

BIKE DOWN A MOUNTAIN?
NO WAY!

That's most everyone's reaction. Mountain biking happens everywhere but the Texas Panhandle. Surprisingly, Amarillo is a hub for some serious MB action with established sites at Palo Duro Canyon State Park, Canyon Trails at Buffalo Hill, and Lake Meredith National Recreation Area. New on the map are the Chad Alan Foster Memorial Trails in Borger, Rick Klein Park in southeast Amarillo, and the Bureau of Land Management's Cross Bar Management Area near the Canadian River. Join the annual 24 Hours in the Canyon ride to raise funds for the local Cancer Survivorship Center. Not a mountain biker but want to feel the thrill? Do a YouTube search for the Rock Garden Trail in Palo Duro Canyon State Park and ride from the rim to the floor of the canyon, a vertical drop of more than 600 feet, in some hair-raising video. Maybe you'll get hooked. Want to learn more? Follow Facebook's Amarillo Mountain Biking page—group rides are regularly announced on the page.

Facebook.com/groups/1452726314951162

"ROUGH IT" OUTDOORS
WITH THESE CABINS AND TENTS

There's a time to rough it in the outdoors. But there's also a time when you may want a little luxury and TLC. The area has several ways to do that in and around Palo Duro Canyon State Park. Doves Rest Resort is 15 cabins on the rim of Palo Duro Canyon, just outside the state park. Nightly rates start at $250, and all the facilities are first-class—many may be the home of your dreams. A night or a weekend is a great way to rest, relax, and socially distance. Palo Duro Glamping is a new offering on the floor of the canyon in the state park. These are high-end tent sites that are fully equipped (even with A/C) and placed in the middle of the canyon. There are only four of these glamping sites. Finally, consider the three rim cabins offered in Palo Duro Canyon State Park. Stone structures built by the CCC in the 1930s, they have been restored and renovated for the modern visitor. Each has a private patio with a view to die for.

Doves Rest Cabins
806-557-8998
dovesrestcabins.com

Palo Duro Glamping
806-488-2821
paloduroglamping.com

Palo Duro Canyon State Park Rim Cabins
512-389-8900
texasstateparks.reserveamerica.com

COLOR YOUR WORLD
DURING A PANHANDLE SUNRISE OR SUNSET

Unless you're at Palo Duro Canyon (southeast of Amarillo) or along the Canadian River (north of Amarillo), it's flat around the Texas Panhandle. There are jokes involving mythical sheriffs and escaped prisoners who rely on the flat horizon. That's all a spatial, three-dimensional thing. It's anything but flat at two special times each day: sunrise and sunset. Then, the Texas Panhandle becomes a fiery blast of reds, oranges, and yellows, combined with the cooling depth of blues, purples, and black. High clouds become mirrors and make the event more dramatic. There's a Facebook group, Panhandle Sunrises and Sunsets, that features nature's paintings with new postings every single day. Enjoy a sunrise or sunset from anywhere, like a Walmart parking lot, Cadillac Ranch, or the hotel window. Better yet, find a field with a classic windmill and just wait. Capture it with your cell phone camera and share with family and friends.

RIDE A HORSE
WITH THESE AREA OUTFITTERS

Every wannabe cowpuncher wants to ride a horse. Amarillo has great choices for you and the entire family. Cowgirls and Cowboys in the West, one of Tripadvisor's top-rated attractions, is one of the best outfitters in the Amarillo area. About 45 minutes southeast of Amarillo on the Los Cedros Ranch, Phyllis Nickum Golden and her team (mostly female) welcome riders of all abilities for morning and afternoon rides (weather permitting). The visit includes simple instructions for everyone, and then the chance to ride up to the rim of Palo Duro Canyon. It's a once-in-a-lifetime opportunity.

Other outfitters, all located in or just outside Palo Duro Canyon State Park, include Palo Duro Stables, Old West Stables, and Palo Duro Creek Ranch. Don't want to ride a horse? Ask the folks at Palo Duro Creek Ranch about four-wheel-drive tours of the canyon.

TIP

During the summer, consider limiting these activities to the morning, especially if you may be on the floor of the canyon. Always carry lots of water.

Cowgirls and Cowboys in the West
19100 FM 1258, 806-672-9256
cowgirlsandcowboysinthewest.com

Old West Stables
11450 Park Rd. 5, Canyon, TX, 806-488-2180
oldweststables.com

Palo Duro Creek Ranch
11301 TX Hwy. 217, Canyon, TX, 806-488-2100
paloduroranch.com

Palo Duro Riding Stables
10160 TX Hwy. 217, Canyon, TX, 806-488-2799
paloduroridingstables.com

RIDE FOR THE BRAND
DURING THE WORLD CHAMPIONSHIP RANCH RODEO

It's the real deal every November in Amarillo. Cowboys from across the US (and sometimes Canada) gather for the World Championship Ranch Rodeo. This 25-year celebration of cowboy culture shows the city folk what it means to ride horseback for a living. Events focus on regular ranch activities, such as wild bronc riding, team penning, team doctoring, and team branding. You have not lived until you watch cowboys sprint the length of a rodeo arena during the Wild Cow Milking event. If you have a cowboy hat and boots, wear them. If not, find them from one of the vendors at the rodeo. It's one time that jeans and pearl-button shirts are the norm, especially when they're creased. Proceeds go to the Working Ranch Cowboy Foundation, offering cowboys and their families "a hand up, not a handout."

408 SW 7th Ave., 806-374-9722
wrca.org/wcrr/

TIP

There are other great rodeos in Amarillo. Try the Coors Cowboy Club Ranch Rodeo in June; the Will Rogers Range Riders Rodeo in July; the Boys Ranch Rodeo over Labor Day weekend; and the Tri-State Fair Professional Rodeo Cowboys Association Rodeo in September.

PEEK OVER THE RIM
INTO PALO DURO CANYON STATE PARK

It's 1890 and your family is moving across the Texas Panhandle by horse-drawn wagon. Suddenly, the flat ground drops away, and a chasm 800 feet deep and a mile wide is staring you in the face. It's Palo Duro Canyon, the Grand Canyon of Texas. Your family has to figure a way around it—not easy, as it extends for over 100 miles. Today, you can drive your family to Palo Duro Canyon State Park, just 25 miles southeast of Amarillo, for an afternoon excursion or extended outdoor adventure. Camping, hiking, mountain biking, horseback riding, picnicking, wildlife viewing, and more await everyone in this very popular, 30,000-acre state park. The Visitor Center and Canyon Gallery are on the rim, and the gallery is operated by the friends of the state park. All proceeds stay in Palo Duro Canyon State Park. The Trading Post on the canyon floor has basic camping supplies, as well as a grill with some of the best burgers around. The park is open, but some COVID-19 restrictions may be in force—call or check online in advance.

11450 Park Rd. 5, Canyon, TX, 806-488-2227
tpwd.texas.gov/state-parks/palo-duro-canyon

TIP

Summer temperatures on the canyon floor routinely exceed 100 degrees. Morning hikes are preferred. Always have plenty of water on hand, wear sunscreen, and take frequent rests.

CULTURE AND HISTORY

STOP AND SMELL THE FLOWERS
IN THE AMARILLO BOTANICAL GARDENS

Set amid the semi-arid Texas Panhandle is an oasis of color and fragrance that will surprise you—the Amarillo Botanical Gardens. More than four acres of lushly planted and beautifully designed gardens offer a respite from the daily humdrum. The spring display features irises, tulips, daffodils, and other blooming bulbs. All moms visit for free on Mother's Day. Be sure to visit the tranquil Japanese Gardens and drop by the Mary Bivins Tropical Conservatory, filled with orchids and tropical plants that contrast Amarillo's climate all year. Christmas lights up with hundreds of thousands of Christmas lights, and Thursday evenings in the summer are filled with Music in the Gardens. Step outside the garden, and you're next to one of the city's best splash pads and playgrounds. Medi-Park Lake is just down the hill, and the Don Harrington Discovery Center is across the parking lot.

1400 Streit Dr., 806-352-6513
amarillobotanicalgardens.org

DON'T HORSE AROUND
AT THE AMERICAN QUARTER HORSE
HALL OF FAME & MUSEUM

As in don't forget to get by the American Quarter Horse Hall of Fame & Museum. The world-class museum is a tribute to the horses and men and women who shaped America from east to west, frequently in the saddle. Hundreds of humans and horses have their names and biographies in the museum's Grand Hall. Don't miss special exhibits in the Scharbauer Gallery, such as the annual America's Horse in Art. Be sure to visit the Hall of Fame exhibit in the back of the building to get a perspective of the American Quarter Horse and the accomplishments of its inductees over time. The museum has been closed during most of the COVID-19 pandemic, but hopes to reopen by the end of 2021. If not, check out its virtual tour. The headquarters of the American Quarter Horse Association is next door to the museum.

2601 I-40 E, 806-376-5181
aqha.com/museum-overview

UNCOVER
AMARILLO'S HORSES OF MANY COLORS

Who says Amarillo is a one-horse town? Not so. We are home to the largest collection of public art horses in the nation, probably the world. Hoof Prints of the American Quarter Horse has brought the beauty of the horse to the streets in over 100 locations around Amarillo. Each horse is sponsored by a local business or person and has a different artist commissioned to complete it. The fiberglass statues turn into incredible works of art, as tributes to the importance of the horse to Amarillo's past, present, and future. The project gets its horsepower from Center City of Amarillo, and you can find a virtual tour of all horse locations on their website. The title sponsor is the American Quarter Horse Association. Speaking of the AQHA, have you been there?

1000 S Polk St., 806-372-6744
centercity.org/hoof-prints

THINK SMALL BUT EXPERIENCE BIG
WHEN VISITING CANADIAN, TEXAS

On the list of best small towns in Texas (however you define that), chances are good you will find Canadian, Texas, a thriving and proud community in Hemphill County about 100 miles northeast of Amarillo. Canadian gets it, with historical restorations, festivals, and (surprise!) a world-class art collection. Check out The Citadelle, a restored historic mansion that is now mentioned with the best art museums in the state. Downtown is a beautiful collection of buildings and businesses (don't miss the restored Palace Theatre). Just north of town is the historic Canadian River Wagon Bridge, which is now a pleasant one-mile hike or bike ride. Drop by Canadian in October for the annual Fall Foliage Festival. The cottonwood trees lining the Canadian River and foliage surrounding Lake Marvin make this a real contender for the best fall colors in Texas.

119 N 2nd St., Canadian, TX, 806-323-6234
canadiantx.org/index.php

SORT THROUGH AMARILLO'S HISTORY
IN ITS CHURCHES

If it's Sunday, don't go back under the covers—consider going to church. With over 300 houses of worship, Amarillo has lots of options, some very surprising. Start with the historic downtown churches, each of which played a part in Amarillo's settling. Consider the east side of town where, chances are, you'll hear the service in a foreign language. Black churches anchor the city's North Side, including the church Oprah frequented during her 1998 trial in Amarillo. Looking for something informal? Try a cowboy church around town. Don't want to stay for a service? Check out the stained glass, church art, and organs located around Amarillo. Not here on a Sunday? Give the church a call and see if they'll let you step inside. A quick Google search will help you sort it out.

TIP

The Catholic Diocese of Amarillo maintains a small museum at its office in northeast Amarillo. 4512 NE 24th Ave., 806-383-2243 amarillodiocese.org/museum-archives.

Historic Downtown Churches

Central Church of Christ
1401 S Madison St., 806-373-4389

First Baptist Church
1208 S Tyler St., 806-373-2891

First Presbyterian Church
1100 S Harrison St., 806-373-4242

Polk St. United Methodist Church
1401 S Polk St., 806-374-2891

St. Mary's Catholic Cathedral
1200 S Washington St., 806-376-7204

VISIT THE DINOSAURS
AT THE DON HARRINGTON
DISCOVERY CENTER

Getting inside the Don Harrington Discovery Center (DHDC) may be the hard part. Kids of all ages will want to hang out with the life-size animatronic dinosaurs in the outdoor science park. Inside, you'll find special traveling exhibits, great permanent exhibits, and the area's only space theater. The digital space shows, many produced locally, bring planets, galaxies, and stars in to your lap. DHDC loves hosting special events, such as Discover for a Dollar, birthday parties with Discovery Center staff to lead the fun and learning, and the Coffee & Cuties programs on first Fridays. So, always check the website or ask at the front desk. Belong to a science museum in your hometown? Ask about reciprocal programs offering reduced admission. When you're done, Medi-Park Lake is just down the hill, the Amarillo Botanical Gardens is across the parking lot, and a splash pad and playground are between.

1200 Streit Dr., 806-355-9547
dhdc.org

CELEBRATE HELIUM
AT THE HELIUM MONUMENT

Between the Don Harrington Discovery Center and the Amarillo Botanical Gardens, it's hard to miss the Helium Monument, a 60-foot-tall, stainless-steel complex of columns. It was placed in Amarillo in 1968 to celebrate the centennial of the discovery of helium. The monument includes four time capsules holding books, artifacts, and documents from 1968—two of the capsules have been opened (1993 and 2018). The Helium Monument is part of the Don Harrington Discovery Center, which maintains a small exhibit about helium. The world's largest helium reserve is in the Cliffside gas field, just a few miles northwest of Amarillo. The Amarillo Helium Plant, inactive since 1998, still stands along Interstate 40 West, near the aptly named Helium Road.

1200 Streit Dr., 806-355-9547
dhdc.org

TIP
Take a careful look at the monument's structure.
It mimics the atomic structure of helium.

CRUISE THE MOTHER ROAD
ACROSS POTTER COUNTY

Cruising, in a car sense, implies a road trip of some length. But cruising in Amarillo may be just 30 miles—about the length of Historic Route 66 as it crosses Potter County. Once the main street of America, and for a time the principal highway linking Amarillo to the outside world, it brought people from all over to town. It still does. Millions of people, particularly Europeans, love the Route 66 culture. Amarillo's Route 66 is anchored by the original location of the Big Texan Steak Ranch on the east side of town and the mother of public art installations, Cadillac Ranch, on the west. However, it's not an authentic Route 66 visit to Amarillo without catching the Historic Route 66 neighborhood along Southwest Sixth Avenue between Georgia and Western streets. It's full of shops (crafts, antiques, interior decorating, biker accessories), galleries, restaurants, and lots of live music venues.

amarillo66.com

TAKE A SELFIE
AT THE "I AM ROUTE 66" PROJECT

A new way to start your Route 66 visit in Amarillo is the Texas Route 66 Visitor Center, home of the "I Am Route 66" photo and book project. Housed in an old building that was an iconic Amarillo restaurant, it is more than a visitor center. It includes art and ideas from the floors to the walls to the exterior. Artist/photographer Jim Livingston houses his "I Am Route 66" photos and interviews in the building, more than 100 dramatic, black and white images with the ordinary people who make Route 66 a travel icon. You'll also see art by other Route 66 artisans from Illinois to California. Look at the new welcome mural on the east side of the building and pose for your Instagram selfie. Staff are always there to answer questions. It's more than a kick!

1900 SW 6th Ave., 806-310-9503
iamrt66.com

LOOK FOR MURALS—
THEY'RE EVERYWHERE

A sharp visitor can tell that Amarillo is home to a growing number of outdoor murals: from small ones along alleys off Historic Route 66 to large ones covering an entire wall in downtown. They're the culmination of hard work and inspiration by artists and civic leaders, something to admire even when driving by. They make outstanding backdrops for selfies, Tik-Toks, and other forms of digital self-expression, while adding color to previously subdued red, brown, and gray walls. Murals are the ultimate 24/7/365 attraction. The Amarillo Convention and Visitors Bureau has built a database of murals and art installations across Amarillo. Take a look at visitamarillo.com/things-to-do/arts/art-installations.

TIP
If the weather drives you indoors, check the murals at the Panhandle-Plains Historical Museum or the J. Marvin Jones Federal Building.

2019 Hoodoo Mural Festival Mural Locations
300 SW 7th Ave.
212 SW 6th Ave.
509 S Tyler St.
414 S Polk St.
406 S Polk St.
411 S Fillmore St.

Route 66 Murals
The Heart of America (it's faded), side of 6th St. Massacre
Haunted House
Welcome to Amarillo, 1900 SW 6th Ave.
About 20 other murals along Historic Route 66

City of Amarillo-Sponsored Murals
Inside passenger terminal, Rick Husband Amarillo
International Airport
1200 S Taylor St.
2406 SW 3rd Ave.
3405 S Western St.
3100 SW 6th Ave.
10th St. underpass between Grant and Garfield streets

Indoor Murals
Panhandle-Plains Historical Museum, 2401 4th Ave., Canyon, TX
J. Marvin Jones Federal Bldg., 205 SE 5th Ave.

TRADE SOME LAND
AT THE XIT MUSEUM

Back in the 1850s, Texas was short of cash but not of land. So, to get the state capitol built in Austin, the state traded roughly three million acres of Panhandle land, where Texas bordered New Mexico. Thousands of acres were developed into the XIT Ranch, a massive ranch that stretched for more than 200 miles and ran over 150,000 cattle. You'll find remnants of the XIT in lots of places (such as Channing and Farwell), but none are better than the XIT Museum in Dalhart. This free museum documents the short life of the XIT, and therefore Dallam and Hartley counties. It's a short drive northwest from Amarillo. During the first long weekend in August, Dalhart celebrates the XIT Rodeo and Reunion, featuring a free barbecue feed bigger than any other.

108 E 5th St., Dalhart, TX, 806-244-5390
xitmuseum.com

GET SOME KICKS
AT SHAMROCK'S U-DROP INN

You've already seen the U-Drop Inn if you watched the original movie, *Cars*. It was Ramone's Paint and Body Shop in mythical Radiator Springs. In real life, it was a gas station and remains one of the best-preserved 1930s buildings along the entire 2,500-mile length of Route 66. It is in Shamrock, just 90 miles east of Amarillo. The neon light from the restored Conoco gas station can be seen for miles. The U-Drop includes a fine little museum and visitor center, as well as Tesla charging stations around back. While in Shamrock, check out the piece of the Blarney Stone, located in Water Tower Park. Better yet, drop by in March for Texas's official St. Patrick's Day Festival, including a beard-growing contest, beauty pageant, parade, and great musical entertainment.

111 US Rt. 66, Shamrock, TX, 806-256-2501
facebook.com/udropinn66

SALUTE OUR HEROES
AT THE TEXAS PANHANDLE WAR MEMORIAL

Amarillo is patriotic. The city is proud of all those who have served the country, especially those who gave their lives during wartime. The Texas Panhandle War Memorial (TPWM), started in 1992, is a beautiful park honoring all our military personnel, and it includes memorials to nine wars and conflicts, from the Spanish-American War through Afghanistan. The names of more than 1,550 Panhandle residents who died in combat during those engagements are engraved on the monuments. Inside the TPWM building are resources expressly for active military, veterans, and their families. Don't miss a large piece of the side and deck of the USS *Arizona,* bombed and sunk during the attack on Pearl Harbor, on outdoor display in the park. It represents a significant moment in our history, and is a magnificent addition to the TPWM.

4111 S Georgia St., 806-350-8387
texaspanhandlewarmemorial.com

FLY WITHOUT LEAVING THE GROUND
AT THE TEXAS AIR & SPACE MUSEUM

Is your head in the clouds, dreaming of flying? From classic aircraft to jets to space, all you want to do is fly. You can dream to your heart's content at the Texas Air & Space Museum, a gem of a collection tucked into a hangar on the edge of Rick Husband Amarillo International Airport. Look for the small white door on the left of the TAC Air hangar. Inside is a surprising collection of aircraft, highlighted by the DC-3/C-47 aircraft that is one of the few operating aircraft on the National Register of Historic Places. Don't miss the rooms of historic uniforms, scale models, and artifacts about flying in Amarillo. Since you're already here, drive over to the ticket lobby of Rick Husband Amarillo International Airport for the exhibit about Amarillo resident Rick Husband, commander of the Space Shuttle *Columbia* that disintegrated on re-entry in February 2003.

10001 American Dr., 806-335-9159
texasairandspacemuseum.org/

FIND AN ARROW
ALONG THE QUANAH PARKER TRAIL

Quanah Parker is another of those bigger-than-life personalities who populated the Amarillo area in the 1800s. He was the last chief of the Comanche Indians—specifically, the Kwahadi tribe that favored Palo Duro Canyon as its home. His tribe avoided contact with the US Army until the Battle of Palo Duro on September 28, 1874. After the tribe's "surrender" in 1875, he began a second life as statesman for the Comanche Indians and developed a close friendship with rancher Charles Goodnight that lasted until they both died in the 1900s. Parker's life is remembered through more than fifty, 22-foot-tall, stylized Comanche arrow sculptures, each commemorating a milestone in his incredible life. Find local arrows at Wildcat Bluff Nature Center and Palo Duro Canyon.

More than 50 locations across the Texas Panhandle, 800-930-6024
quanahparkertrail.com

STROLL THROUGH
THE PANHANDLE-PLAINS
HISTORICAL MUSEUM

Texas is full of them: things that are big. Canyon has one of note—the Panhandle-Plains Historical Museum. It's the largest history museum in Texas. It's so big (over two million artifacts—too many for all to be on display at the same time) that some call it The Smithsonian with a Texas accent. It's that good, too. History, geology, paleontology, fine art, Native American art and artifacts, oil and gas history. It's all here. Established in the 1920s and built with public donations during the Great Depression, it has something for everyone. Maybe it's the windmill collection featuring the machine that irrigated the Great Plains. And don't miss the fine art collection that includes an original by Georgia O'Keeffe. Even paying admission is memorable—look up when you're at the entrance desk and see eight murals by Harold Bugbee or Ben Carlton Mead around the top of Pioneer Hall that outline hundreds of years of local history.

2401 4th Ave., Canyon, 806-651-2244
panhandleplains.org

SEE THE LIGHT
FROM POLK STREET'S NEON SIGNS

Polk Street was Amarillo's main drag for decades. High schoolers cruised on Friday and Saturday nights. Families shopped in downtown department stores. People went to movie theaters and restaurants that lined the street. Back in the 1940s, it was named the best-lit street in America. Relive that era by walking or driving between 10th and Sixth avenues to see the wide variety of neon signs restored along Polk. The old Paramount Theater sign on the south end and the new Amarillo National Bank sign on the north end frame other signs for the Courtyard by Marriott, Kress, The Barfield, Crush, Six Car, and even the restored (but unlit) F.W. Woolworth facade at Seventh and Polk. It's a simple and free way to enjoy an evening walk or cruise along Polk Street.

DANCE
WITH THE KWAHADIS

The Kwahadi Dancers never disappoint. These young men and women, all members of a local scout Venture Crew, are consummate performers dedicated to preserving the dance, music, culture, and history of Native Americans. They make their own costumes, rehearse long hours, and travel across the Panhandle and around the country. Performances, in a non-pandemic world, are spaced across the calendar. The winter show is usually in January and February, and the summer show is in either June or July, depending on their travel schedule. Admission includes the fantastic museum (don't miss the Thomas Mails collection), as well as the performances. When there is no show slated, the museum is open on Saturday and Sunday afternoons. The Trading Post includes some of the best Native American arts and crafts in the Panhandle, and sales help them "keep the lights on."

9151 I-40 E, 806-335-3175
kwahadi.com

ADD KENNETH WYATT
TO YOUR ART COLLECTION

Serious collectors of Western and Christian art will know the name Kenneth Wyatt. A Panhandle native, Wyatt is a gifted speaker, ordained minister, published author, and a talented painter. His work mirrors rural life, from roundups to courtin' to thunderstorms, and is available as original art, reproductions, cards, and other products. His Christian art reflects his deep personal feelings. Churches of all denominations, from Texas to around the world, have reproductions of his moving paintings of the apostles. "I just push around the paint until it looks like what I see inside," Wyatt says. His entire family is artistically talented, producing paintings, sculptures, jewelry, and more. The family also has galleries in Tulia, Texas (his home), and in Red River and Ruidoso, New Mexico.

7306 SW 34th Ave., Ste. 12, 806-803-9265
kennethwyatt.com

STAY IN THE WEST
WITH JACK SORENSON'S PAINTINGS

Jack Sorenson grew up in Palo Duro Canyon—literally. His childhood was spent on the rim of the canyon, and many weekends were devoted to exploring its walls. Artistically gifted since childhood, he sold out his first show in 1974. Since then, Sorenson committed to a creative life that drew on his Western roots. He painted hundreds of Western scenes, from the depths of Palo Duro Canyon to high in the Rocky Mountains. His work is available as an original piece of art or as high-quality prints. Also, his images have appeared on magazine covers, on a popular series of Leanin' Tree greeting cards, and on popular jigsaw puzzles. He runs all queries on his artwork through his website, but he welcomes the chance for a special showing. Just contact him and give him a few days to put something together.

jacksorensonfineart.com

TAKE THE BUS
TO FIND LOCAL ART AT THE GREYHOUND GALLERY

It was a happening place for Amarillo in the 1940s: 814 South Taylor Street. It's where you caught a Greyhound bus to head home or to go see a boyfriend or girlfriend, or just to go see the big world. Now, it's a new stop on the area's art scene—the Greyhound Gallery. Its opening show in early 2021 was dedicated to the creative spirit found among many young residents. Renovated to be an event space as well as a gallery, its sleek interior is as much part of the art as the items on the walls. Give them a call or check their Facebook page to see what's hanging in the gallery.

814 S Taylor St., 806-318-4119
greyhoundgallery.com

TIP

Drop by the Cerulean Gallery, now located just a few blocks away in the Embassy Suites Downtown at 550 S Buchanan Street. Since it is in the public areas of the hotel, the Cerulean is always open.

RELIVE THE HIGH LIFE
AT THE RV MUSEUM

Some visitors say it is the best museum in Amarillo. Now, it is in the newest facility in town. The Jack Sisemore Traveland RV Museum, chronicling America's love affair with the outdoors, whether from a camper, recreational vehicle, motorcycle, or boat, has moved to a bigger, better building just a few miles down the road. This private collection is now at 14500 I-27. It still features the oldest Airstream trailer, several rare and historic RVs, some classic motorcycles, a wood-sided Chris-Craft motorboat, a replica of Jack Sisemore's first gas station, and timely accessories that have been donated by individuals or collected by the Sisemores. Now, more items in the collection can be displayed. Best of all, the museum is free. Cross your fingers: you may bump into owners Jack (father) or Trent (son) Sisemore and get to visit face-to-face.

14501 I-27, 806-690-3377
rvmuseum.net

READ THE ROAD SIGNS
INSTALLED BY THE DYNAMITE MUSEUM

Hey, did that road sign say, "I'm Still Alive?" What about that one? It reads, "Art Is What You Can Get Away With." That one reads, "Road Does Not End." What gives? Just what are these signs, and who put them here? Local legend traces them to Stanley Marsh 3, the man behind Cadillac Ranch, and a collective of local artists called the Dynamite Museum charged with imagining, designing, executing, and installing them all over Amarillo. There are hundreds of signs (there may have been 1,000 or more), all diamond-shaped to mimic warning road signs, although none conflict with official yellow warning signs. Most are on private property. Keep your eyes open, especially along Historic Route 66, South Washington Street, and East Amarillo Boulevard.

facebook.com/thedynamitemuseum

PAINT A CAR
AT THE CADILLAC RANCH

There are no signs pointing to it, but over 1.5 million folks stop here each year—cold or hot, rain or snow. Located in a farmer's field just a few miles west of Amarillo, Cadillac Ranch has been fascinating visitors since 1974. Local eccentric millionaire Stanley Marsh 3 worked with San Francisco-based art group The Ant Farm to develop and install this unique collection of 10 Cadillacs buried nose-first in the ground. Marsh said it was dedicated to the golden age of the American car. It has become the most visible example of public art in the US, and nearly every visitor has left a message on the Cadillacs. In fact, local lore says the nearest Home Depot sells more spray paint than any other big-box hardware store in the nation. Remember, dispose of your spray can properly—don't litter the Ranch. Its 50th anniversary is in 2024. The Marsh family still owns the ranch and hopes to make improvements that will guarantee it continues to draw visitors off Interstate 40 for another 50 years.

13651 I-40 Frontage Rd.
facebook.com/1974cadillacranch

GET HOOKED
AT THE DEVIL'S ROPE MUSEUM

This small, family-run museum may win the best name contest. Since 1991, it has displayed one of the largest private collections of barbed wire in the world. Before the invention of barbed wire, cattle grazed on the open range. Brands were needed to identify cattle, and large roundups were used to collect, sort, doctor, brand, and move cattle. Barbed wire changed the Western landscape overnight. The first area ranch completely surrounded by barbed wire was the Frying Pan Ranch in the mid-1870s, west of present-day Amarillo. Now, barbed wire is used whenever a project demands fencing around big areas. The other half of the small museum is the Route 66 Museum, focusing on the Mother Road as it came through McLean and the Texas Panhandle in the 1920s and 1930s.

100 Kingsley St., McLean, TX, 806-779-2225
barbwiremuseum.com

TIP
Ask about the restored 1929 Route 66 Gas Station
in McLean, just a few blocks away.

GO TO COURT
IN POTTER AND RANDALL COUNTIES

Texas is known for its 254 counties and their 254 county courthouses. These buildings are where big cities grew up, and they remain a focal point of life for smaller cities and towns. Amarillo is the rare city whose boundary crosses into two counties, Potter and Randall. Each county is home to a historic courthouse. The Potter County Courthouse in downtown Amarillo still contains offices and courtrooms for the county's daily business. It is a Prairie Deco design from 1928 that is listed on the National Register of Historic Places. The Randall County Courthouse in Canyon dates to 1909, and an exterior restoration was completed in 2010. County government and business are conducted in other locations, but the courthouse is the center of Canyon's beautiful square. Each building has a state historical marker.

Potter County Courthouse
500 S Fillmore St., 806-379-2246
co.potter.tx.us

Randall County Courthouse
501 E 16th St., Ste. 303, Canyon, TX, 806-468-5500
randallcounty.com/207/County-Judge

BURY THOSE COMBINES AND BUGS
IN THE GROUND

It started with Cadillac Ranch, and since then, Americans across the country have been burying things in the ground and calling it art. But someone brighter than me said imitation is the sincerest form of flattery. There are two examples of such admiration close to Amarillo. Combine City has 14 combines, the Cadillacs of farm equipment, planted in the ground along the Claude Highway (FM 1151), southeast of Amarillo. While barbed wire keeps you from painting the combines a la Cadillac Ranch, it is a place to stop and admire. The Slug Bug Ranch, east of Amarillo along Interstate 40 at Conway, Texas, is a smaller installation, with five Volkswagen Beetles planted nose-first into the ground. Admirers are permitted to leave their marks on the Bug Ranch, too. Maybe all this makes Amarillo the epicenter of buried outdoor sculptures. Then again, maybe it's all just a coincidence. Enjoy.

Combine City, FM 1151 near Whitaker Rd.
atlasobscura.com/places/combine-city

Slug Bug Ranch, I-40, Exit 96, Conway, TX
roadsideamerica.com/story/17024

HOP ON DOWN
TO CANYON

Just 15 miles south of Amarillo is the big, little town of Canyon. Home to West Texas A&M University and gateway to Palo Duro Canyon State Park, Canyon has enjoyed a renaissance. New shops and restaurants fill the storefronts around the historic Randall County Courthouse, itself the focus of a restoration project. Among the town's new and old highlights are Palace Coffee (this local landmark started here), bigger-than-life-size Tex Randall (he has a new coat of paint), El Patio (attracting Tex-Mex fans for years), Panhandle's Rushmore (a new mural in the heart of town), Palo Duro Canyon Outfitters, and Burrowing Owl Books (welcoming readers of all ages). Canyon's Fourth of July celebration attracts more than 20,000 visitors and is one of the best small-town July 4th fairs in the nation.

1518 5th Ave., Canyon, TX, 806-655-7815
canyonchamber.org

HANG ON
AT CAL FARLEY'S BOYS RANCH

Sometimes, you just need a little help. Amarillo businessman and philanthropist Cal Farley knew that. Many young kids growing up in the Great Depression looked for a "shirttail to hang on to." Still do. Drive out of Amarillo about 35 miles northwest to Cal Farley's Boys Ranch on US Highway 385, a sprawling ranch/school/home developed to give kids in a tough jam a place to call home. Since 1936, thousands of boys and girls have graduated from Boys Ranch and succeeded in life. Pre-pandemic visitors were welcome to tour the campus and have lunch with the residents—please call in advance. Labor Day weekend is special at Boys Ranch, with the annual Boys Ranch Rodeo. All the kids look forward to participating in the big event.

US Hwy. 385, Boys Ranch, TX, 800-687-3722
calfarley.org

TIP
Across the highway from Boys Ranch is Boot Hill, the cemetery for old Tascosa, one of the three original towns in the Texas Panhandle.

REV YOUR ENGINES
AT BILL'S BACKYARD CLASSICS

Find a shady tree, and chances are you'll find an owner/backyard mechanic working on a classic car. Now, find Amarillo's tribute to cars and their owners at Bill's Backyard Classics, a collection of over 100 of the best-preserved and best-restored cars in the nation. The brainchild of Bill and Linda Pratt, the collection reaches back to the 1920s and features cars and trucks. Don't miss Bob Seger's Pontiac Catalina convertible or Judge Roy Hofheinz's Cadillac Fleetwood limousine. The collection contains, as Bill would say, "anything that could be fixed under a tree." Bill passed in late 2019, but Linda, his family, and the museum continue his passion for classic cars. Call first to check if the museum is open.

5309 S Washington St., 806-373-8194
bbcamatx.com

WALK ON THE WILD SIDE
THROUGH THE AMARILLO ZOO

Perhaps the best value for its admission price, the Amarillo Zoo covers 14 exciting acres in Amarillo's Thompson Park. The hilltop facility features shaded paths and viewing areas, great for the summer. Zoo species include monkeys, lions, bears, birds, reptiles, and more. Don't miss the native animal display featuring bison, antelope, prairie dogs, and other residents of the Texas Panhandle. Staff are frequently stationed throughout the zoo grounds, with some special activities targeted to younger visitors. The zoo is open daily from 9:30 a.m. to 5 p.m., and admission is 4–3–2: $4 for adults (13–61), $3 for seniors (62 and over), $2 for children (3–12), and free for infants.

700 Comanchero Trail, 806-381-7911
zoo.amarillo.gov

TIP
Call the zoo in advance to determine the best time to visit,
hopefully when the animals are most active.

SOAK UP THE ART
AT THE AMARILLO MUSEUM OF ART

It's three stories of galleries, featuring many artistic styles and media. Changing exhibits and special shows dot the calendar. The permanent collection includes depth and breadth, from more than 300 pieces of priceless Asian art to four pieces by temporary resident Georgia O'Keeffe. One Google review was simply, "OMG, this place is too cool." It is the Amarillo Museum of Art, a treasure on the Amarillo College campus. Admission is always free—donations are welcome. It has modified hours due to the pandemic: Friday and Saturday from 10 a.m. to 5 p.m., and Sunday from noon to 5 p.m.

2200 S Van Buren St., 806-371-5050
amoa.org

TIP
While you're there, look around the main campus of Amarillo College, a hometown favorite and one of the country's best community colleges.

CORRAL AMARILLO'S HISTORY
AT THE AMARILLO LIVESTOCK AUCTION

Cattle are important to Amarillo. In the early 1900s, there were more cattle in and around the city than human residents. Cattle drives trailed up Polk Street to the rail headings on the north side of downtown. The Amarillo Livestock Auction was one of the largest auctions in the nation. In 2020, they still mainly handled cattle but auctioned other livestock, too. Some of the auction business has moved to smaller towns or online. But every Monday at 11 a.m., buyers and sellers meet to keep the business moving. Feel free to stop by and see the auction in person. Get there early to have breakfast or a cup of coffee in Amarillo's Stockyard Grill. Read the historical marker outside the front door. Once the auctioneer starts his patter, keep your hand down, or you may be going home with some cattle.

100 S Manhattan St., 806-373-7464
amarillolivestockauction.com

EXPLORE
THE CARSON COUNTY SQUARE HOUSE MUSEUM

Start with a square house—a small, white clapboard structure that is the oldest building in town. After more than 80 years as a private residence, restore it for the entire county to share. Acquire other historic buildings and complete new exhibit spaces. Fill it with more than 10,000 artifacts from the area, as well as sculptures and art produced by local artists. Get the original square house listed on the National Register of Historic Places, as well as the list of Texas Historic Landmarks. You have the Carson County Square House Museum, the historical ground zero for Carson County, northeast of Amarillo. It's free (donations are always welcome) and located in Panhandle, Texas.

503 Elsie St., Panhandle, TX, 806-537-3524
facebook.com/SquareHouseMuseum

SEE HOW THE ONE PERCENT LIVED
AT THE HARRINGTON HOUSE

It's not how I grew up—probably not you, either. But it's a wonderful look into history, culture, and philanthropy in Amarillo. Don't miss the Harrington House on Polk Street, just south of downtown. Built in 1914 by cattlemen, this fine, neoclassical mansion has over 15,000 square feet of floor space, 20 rooms, eight bathrooms, and seven fireplaces on four levels. The house was acquired by Don and Sybil Harrington in 1940, and their endowment keeps it preserved to this day. The Harringtons' giving across Amarillo—to scouting, the arts, health care, education, and more—is a legacy still seen today. Their home was decorated to the nines and was visited by movie stars and celebrities of the day. Excellent tours are given on Tuesday and Thursday mornings, and some special restrictions apply—be sure to call for reservations and to get all the details.

1600 S Polk St., 806-374-5490
harringtonhousehistorichome.org

STAY
IN A HISTORIC HOTEL

Two of Amarillo's most historic tall buildings now are boutique hotels. The Fisk Building, long the place where Amarilloans went to see a doctor or dentist, is a Courtyard by Marriott. The Fisk opened in 1927, built by Guy Carlander. The Courtyard has modernized the lobby and guest rooms, but has kept a small museum of photos and information on the old building in its lobby. Make sure you see the old elevator equipment preserved in the walkway to the parking garage. The Barfield dates to 1927 and sits at the corner of Polk Street and Route 66. Reopened in April 2021 as part of Marriott's Autograph Collection, it favors the Art Deco design from its heyday. Ask about its modern "speakeasy," accessible through a hidden bookcase. Have questions? Staff of each hotel would be happy to help you.

Courtyard by Marriott Downtown
724 S Polk St., 806-553-4500
marriott.com/hotels/travel/amadt-courtyard-amarillo-downtown

The Barfield
600 S Polk St., 806-414-2200
thebarfield.com

TIP

The Herring Hotel, one of the city's premier destinations, is closed. But ask around—you may get lucky and nab a rare tour of its lobby and the murals in the basement.

CATCH A FLICK
IN A HISTORIC THEATER

It used to be Friday night meant an evening in town and a visit to the movie theater, either with your buddies or with your date. Some theaters had big, bright marquees and neon lights, while others were little more than storefronts. All of them transported viewers to another place and time. All those on this list have been restored and are being used by their communities for concerts, theater companies, community meetings and, yes, even movies. Most don't have events planned every weekend, so it's best to check in advance. It never hurts to bring some popcorn, too.

Historic Theaters Near Amarillo

Morley Theatre (1947)
701 N Main St., Borger, TX
806-274-5000

Texas Theater (1920)
217 N Main St., Shamrock, TX
806-216-0649

Palace Theatre (1909)
210 W Main St., Canadian, TX
806-323-5133

Lyric Cinema (1948)
113 Main St., Spearman, TX
806-644-2812

Mulkey Theatre (1946)
106 Kearney St., Clarendon, TX
806-874-7469

Royal Theatre (1948)
118 SE 2nd St., Tulia, TX
806-995-4000

Gem Theatre (1915)
120 Trice St., Claude, TX
806-226-2187

Gem Theatre (1928)
217 Main St., Turkey, TX
806-423-1420

La Rita Theatre (1928)
311 Denrock Ave., Dalhart, TX
806-224-6222

Ritz Theatre (1928)
902 East Ave., Wellington, TX
806-447-0090

Ellis Theater (1928)
217 S Main St., Perryton, TX
806-435-4133

TAKE A WALK
ON POLK STREET

Amarillo's main drag was Polk Street. It's where you went to shop, to the doctor, out to eat, to the movies, to school, to work, and even to cruise. It has enjoyed a rebirth in the past 10 years, but always with an eye to its history. Take a walk from Third Avenue south to 16th Avenue for a lesson about Amarillo's heyday. The Bivins Building at 418 South Polk was home to the electric utility. The oldest commercial building in downtown Amarillo may be at 500 South Polk—look down at the foundation stonework to get an inkling of its age. The Kress Building at 702 South Polk features some beautiful Pueblo Deco details. The Paramount Theatre was one of the movie houses on Polk. The sign was restored and returned to its original location, and it's beautiful at night. The Bivins Mansion, at 1000 South Polk, is a three-story, Georgian-Revival-style house from 1905 that many locals remember as the Amarillo Public Library. The Sharpened Iron Studios at 1314 South Polk was the location of the original Amarillo High School, which was destroyed by fire in 1970. Polk Street United Methodist Church, at 1401 South Polk, was built in 1928. The congregation is the oldest in Amarillo, from 1888. Finish your walk in front of the opulent Harrington House.

TIP
Keep your eye out for state historical markers along Polk Street.

CLIMB ABOARD
THE RAILROAD ALL ACROSS AMARILLO

Amarillo is a railroad town. It is here because two railroads, the Fort Worth & Denver and the Atchison, Topeka & Santa Fe, intersected here in the late 1880s. It's no surprise that the city still relies on the railroad for a large part of its existence. Railroad highlights include the old Santa Fe Depot (401 South Grant Street), now owned by the city and under plans for future redevelopment. The Madame Queen, a 2-10-4 Texas-type locomotive built in 1930 for the Plains Division of the Santa Fe Railway, is displayed at 500 Southeast 2nd Avenue in downtown Amarillo. The Santa Fe Building (900 South Polk Street), owned and renovated by Potter County, glows red with its neon sign nightly. Grab your bike or a pair of good walking shoes for the Rock Island Rail Trail, a five-mile linear park roughly parallel to Plains Boulevard, developed from the right of way of the Rock Island Line.

TIP

Make the drive to the Amarillo Railroad Museum. Volunteers are building an HO scale model of the local rail network, complete with landmarks and highlights. It's open a couple times a month, and a volunteer is always happy to show you around. 3160 I Ave., 806-335-3333, amarillorailmuseum.com

READ THROUGH HISTORY
WITH STATE HISTORICAL MARKERS

Texas state historical markers are one of the Texas Historical Commission's largest and most visible projects. Thousands of markers cover all 254 Texas counties, including Potter and Randall. An afternoon exploring for local historical markers is fun and educational, and they are everywhere. Just a few located in Amarillo include Polk Street United Methodist Church, Polk Street Schools, Amarillo Livestock Auction, Santa Fe Building, Courtyard by Marriott (formerly the Fisk Building), and Potter County Courthouse. Or just stop when you see the sign, Historical Marker One Mile on Left/Right. You never know what you will learn. Want to go to the source? Check out the Texas Historical Commission website. The site offers some search utility, which can be helpful. Don't be fooled by "fake" historical markers—Amarillo's most famous is a look-alike marker at Ozymandias, a large public art creation of Stanley Marsh 3 at Interstate 27 and Sundown Lane.

REFLECT ON LIFE
AT THE CROSS AT GROOM

Looking for a place to take a break, stretch your legs, and clear your mind? The Cross at Groom may be that place. Just 40 miles east of Amarillo, the cross has been welcoming travelers of all backgrounds since 1995. The 190-foot-tall cross is one of the tallest freestanding crosses in the world. It is illuminated at night, making it a beacon for travelers wanting something more than a bathroom break. The grounds also contain a garden, gift shop, theater, and many bronze sculptures that provoke thoughts and encourage meditation. Sunrise and sunset offer extra drama for the traveler, combining breathtaking colors on the horizon with this man-made structure.

I-40, Exit 112, Groom, TX, 806-248-9006
crossministries.net

TIP
Travel to the east side of Groom to see the Leaning Water Tower, an attention-getting device that attracted thousands of cars to the Britten Truck Stop on Route 66: atlasobscura.com/places/the-leaning-tower-of-groom-texas.

FEEL THE DRAMA
UNDER THE STARS AT *TEXAS!*

Ever wondered how this part of the state was settled? Instead of doing a Google search, head to the outdoor musical drama *TEXAS,* held nightly (except Monday) from June to August in Palo Duro Canyon State Park. Watch farmers and ranchers settle the tough land while trying to deal with each other and the Native Americans and Comancheros who already roamed the land. The acting, singing, and dancing are on the mark, and each year the production is tweaked to improve the performance for audiences. Stay in your seats for the fireworks finale. Prices vary with seat location, but admission to the state park after 4 p.m. is always free for *TEXAS* attendees. Curtain (so to speak) is at 8:30 p.m. If you're hungry, ask about the pre-show meal. If you're interested, take a backstage tour before the show. On clear summer nights, you'll see the Milky Way over the canyon. Meet the cast, lined up in the plaza after the show. You'll be happy you did.

Pioneer Amphitheatre
Palo Duro Canyon State Park, 806-655-2181
texas-show.com

ESCAPE AMARILLO
FOR THE GOODNIGHT HISTORICAL CENTER

Charles Goodnight was many things. He was a Texas Ranger in the 1860s. He was a cattleman and, with Oliver Loving, established the Goodnight-Loving Trail, leading Texas cattle to market in Denver. While on one of those trail drives, he may have developed the chuck box, a folding kitchen for early wagons that fed cowboys on the range. With John Adair, he established the JA Ranch, the first ranch in the Texas Panhandle, and drove his first herd of cattle into Palo Duro Canyon in 1876. He founded the town of Goodnight, Texas, about 40 miles southeast of Amarillo, and lived there in a classic two-story ranch home until 1929. The home is now the Charles and Mary Ann Goodnight Ranch State Historic Site. The fully restored home out on the prairie gives us a sense of what it was like to be a Panhandle pioneer. Catch a glimpse of the bison herd next door at Herd Wear Retail Store, a private business dedicated to all things made from bison.

4989 County Rd. 25 (at US 287), Goodnight, TX, 806-944-5591
thc.texas.gov/historic-sites/charles-and-mary-ann-goodnight-ranch-state-historic-site

---

TIP
Don't miss the Goodnight gravesite in the town cemetery across US 287 from the historic home.

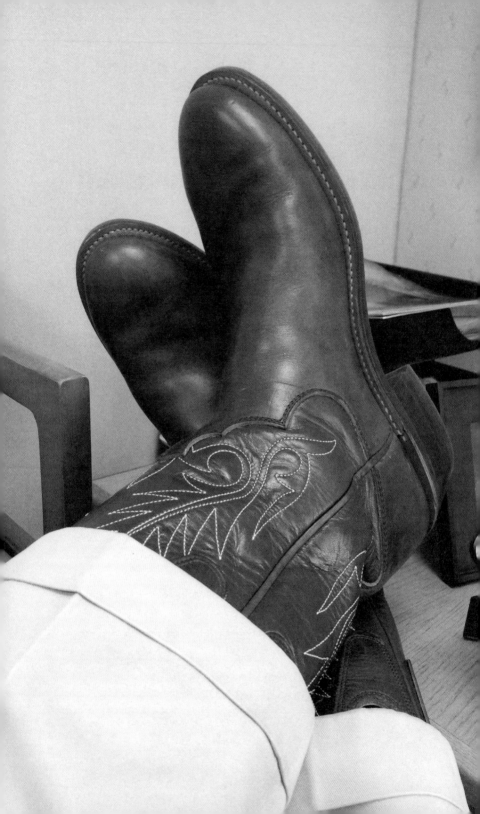

SHOPPING AND FASHION

PICK SOMETHING FRESH
FROM THE AMARILLO COMMUNITY MARKET

Farmers markets have become more than locally grown tomatoes, peppers, and corn. They also feature herbs, local jams and jellies, maybe local eggs and local beef, and of course some local baked goods. Local crafts, too. Where do you find that, with a dose of community spirit, in Amarillo? It's the Amarillo Community Market, each Saturday morning from 8 a.m. to 12:30 p.m., from mid-June to Labor Day weekend. Up to 150 vendors surround the Bivins Mansion (Amarillo's oldest home) at 10th and Polk Street in downtown. You'll bump into families, dogs, musicians, yoga classes, food trucks, and so much more. Remember, local produce starts to come in during July. There is no admission fee—just bring a reusable bag to carry your purchases.

1000 S Polk St., 806-335-6360
amarillocommunitymarket.weebly.com

THINK GLOBAL, SHOP LOCAL
WITH CHALICE ABBEY

Looking for a way to shop around the world while making sure the farmers, craftsmen, and artisans receive a fair price for their goods? Chalice Abbey is the answer. They have jewelry, baskets, pottery, wall hangings, musical instruments, and many other gift ideas from Third-World suppliers. There are also some items from local artists. All sales help support the artists and let the Abbey purchase more fair-trade products. One reviewer calls it "the gift store of the future." Affiliated with the Christian Church of the Southwest, the Abbey also includes the Center for Spirituality and the Arts, which hosts a variety of gatherings, concerts, and art shows. It offers programs on personal transformation, embodied practice, and engaged living.

2717 Stanley St., Ste. A, 806-576-2480
chaliceabbey.org

JUMP INTO THE NAT
ON HISTORIC ROUTE 66

Starting life as Amarillo's swimming pool in 1922, The Nat (short for The Natatorium) is a unique building with a history all its own. It was enclosed and converted to a concert and dance hall. Many big bands stopped here, including Tommy Dorsey, Harry James, Guy Lombardo, Duke Ellington, and Count Basie. After a stint as a private event center, it has become one of Amarillo's best shopping destinations. Today, it is The Nat Antiques & Collectibles on Route 66. Over 100 dealers offer some of the best collectibles and interior accessories found on the Mother Road. As you browse (allow a couple hours), you can find the old stage as well as the balcony from the dance hall days. The building is listed on the National Register of Historic Places (as are many buildings along Amarillo's Historic Route 66), and a state historical marker is right out front.

2705 SW 6th Ave., 806-367-8908
thenatroute66.com

SHOP, EAT, PLAY, AND SLEEP
IN TOWN SQUARE VILLAGE

Amarillo has some great neighborhoods for eating and shopping. Here's one that's brand new—Town Square Village. On the far southwest edge of town, it's a large multibuilding complex that visitors love for shopping and eating options. Upscale dining has taken Town Square by storm. The Metropolitan has developed a loyal clientele that loves its jazzy, classic lines and menu. Cask & Cork's rooftop patio is famous for sunsets and great drinks. Awaken Spa, Verdure, and Town Square Nutrition help with your well-being. Have fun at Cinergy (games, movies, escape room, bowling alley, and laser arcade) and Amp'd, a trampoline park with a climbing wall and much more. Come at Christmas, when the lights focus on a 40-foot-tall tree in the center of the village. Don't want to leave? The top floors feature some of Amarillo's most exciting apartment options.

9181 Town Sq. Blvd., 806-404-0595
townsquareliving.com

SMELL THE LEATHER
AT OLIVER SADDLE SHOP

What's your favorite aroma? Coffee? Flowers? Perfume? Anything on the grill? What smells the very best? An answer may be leather. Newly tanned, hand-tooled, well-cared-for leather. Walk into Oliver Saddle Shop (more than 100 years in Amarillo), and that aroma surrounds you. Why? In the back room are several workbenches, each manned by a member of the Oliver family, building saddles, chaps, belts, and other important tack that is vital cowboy equipment. Some Oliver saddles are in the same family 50 years. Need something else handcrafted in leather, maybe a hand-tooled briefcase? Ask them about it—chances are they can help you out. Not a cowboy? They've worked on saddles and tack for wannabes too, like President George W. Bush. Don't expect to walk out with your new saddle—their craftsmanship takes three to five months, depending on the backlog.

3016 Plains Blvd., 806-372-7562
oliversaddle.com

SHOP IN AN RV PARK
AT LIZZIE MAE'S MERCANTILE

One of Amarillo's best, and certainly most surprising, shopping destinations is Lizzie Mae's Mercantile. You'll find cabin, RV, and home décor as well as jewelry, candles, pillows, purses, Willow Tree collectibles, Texas-themed items, locally crafted honey butter, salsa, and other food items. The Christmas Shop—open year-round—is second to none. The 3,000-square-foot mercantile cabin is located at Fort Amarillo RV & Resort—that's the surprise. The Prescott family is behind the RVs and Lizzie Mae's, making both great places to stop since the 1980s.

10101 Business I-40 W, 806-331-1710
lizziemaes.net

POLISH YOUR IMAGE
WITH CADILITE JEWELRY FROM LILE ART GALLERY

One of your stops should be Cadillac Ranch. Take a can of spray paint along (better yet, use a can you find on the ground) and add to the layers of artwork. Now, think about how thick the coats of spray paint have become. What could you do with it? To find out one man's answer, cruise down to the Lile Art Gallery on Historic Route 66, say hello to social watchdogs Lady and Zeek, and make yourself at home with Bob Lile, creator of Cadilite jewelry. He uses old paint chips that have fallen off cars at the Cadillac Ranch (he does not take them off the cars) and polishes and buffs until he finds some color combination he likes. The result is some of the smartest-looking earrings, necklaces, and bracelets around. "Croc," as he is known to friends and strangers alike, also has been up and down the entire length of Route 66 numerous times, and he can help you with any Mother Road question.

2719 SW 6th Ave., 806-664-3089
facebook.com/Cadilite

THROW A POT,
BUT NOT AT SOMEONE,
AT BLUE SAGE GALLERY

Kent and Megan Harris are serious about pottery. They handcraft high-quality pottery for the home, kitchen, and garden. Some of Amarillo's newest and hippest restaurants use their plates. They also are part of a younger group of artists starting to make their homes and businesses along Historic Route 66. Kent and Megan also offer a wide array of classes, from beginner to more advanced, because there is nothing like getting a little clay under your fingernails. But walking around their gallery, filled with natural light, is a fine way to enjoy a day.

3300-3302 SW 6th St., 806-282-2275
bluesagepottery.com

DESIGN YOUR BOOTS
AT BECK COWBOY BOOTS

I took a New York City writer to Beck Cowboy Boots once—
she wanted an interview for a story on celebrities and boots.
She asked then-owner Harry Beck, "Which celebrities have you
made boots for?" His answer: "All our celebrities are cowboys.
Working cowboys. People making their living from the back
of a horse." Fast-forward a few years. Beck Cowboy Boots is
still here (unfortunately, Harry isn't), handcrafting boots for
cowboys as well as many other folk—maybe you. Stop in for a
visit, maybe some measurements (including a full cast of your
foot), and pick out your leather, color, and trim. Your handmade
boots, with great style, fit, and durability, will be ready in a few
weeks. I love my pair of Beck boots!

723 S Georgia St., 806-373-1600
beckboots.com

Photo by Ralph Duke

ACTIVITIES
BY SEASON

SPRING

SUMMER

FALL

WINTER

SUGGESTED
ITINERARIES

GET SOME KICKS ON ROUTE 66

Devour a Classic Burger at the GoldenLight Café, 2

Eat a Steak (What Else?) at the Big Texan Steak Ranch, 17

Take a Selfie at the "I Am Route 66" Project, 83

Get Some Kicks at Shamrock's U-Drop Inn, 87

Paint a Car at the Cadillac Ranch, 100

Jump into The Nat on Historic Route 66, 126

Polish Your Image with Cadilite Jewelry from Lile Art Gallery, 130

Throw a Pot, but Not at Someone, at Blue Sage Gallery, 131

SO MANY MUSEUMS, NOT ENOUGH TIME

Don't Horse Around at the American Quarter Horse Hall of Fame & Museum, 75

Visit the Dinosaurs at the Don Harrington Discovery Center, 80

Relive the High Life at the RV Museum, 98

Stroll Through the Panhandle-Plains Historical Museum, 91

Rev Your Engines at Bill's Backyard Classics, 106

See How the One Percent Lived at the Harrington House, 111

FREE (DONATIONS ARE ALWAYS WELCOME)

Listen to Summer Music Festivals in Amarillo and Canyon, 42

Search for History in Alibates Flint Quarries National Monument, 50

Color Your World During a Panhandle Sunrise or Sunset, 65

INDEX